100 THINGS
You Don't Know About
ATLANTIC
CANADA
For Kids

SARAH SAWLER

NIMBUS
PUBLISHING
— NIMBUS.CA —

*For Simon, who never runs out of
stories to tell (or questions to ask)*

Nimbus Publishing Limited
3660 Strawberry Hill St, Halifax, NS, B3K 5A9
(902) 455-4286 nimbus.ca

Printed and bound in Canada
Cover and interior design: John van der Woude, JVDW Designs
NB1285

Library and Archives Canada Cataloguing in Publication

   Sawler, Sarah, author
   100 things you don't know about Atlantic Canada (for kids) / Sarah Sawler.
   Includes bibliographical references.
   Issued in print and electronic formats.
   ISBN 978-1-77108-567-0 (softcover).—ISBN 978-1-77108-568-7(HTML)
   1. Atlantic Provinces—History—Miscellanea—Juvenile literature. 2. Atlantic Provinces—Miscellanea—Juvenile literature. I. Title. II. Title: One hundred things you do not know about Atlantic Canada.

FC2005.S29 2018   j971.5002   C2017-907921-2
                                 C2017-907922-0

Nimbus Publishing acknowledges the financial support for its publishing activities from the Government of Canada through the Canada Book Fund (CBF) and the Canada Council for the Arts, and from the Province of Nova Scotia. We are pleased to work in partnership with the Province of Nova Scotia to develop and promote our creative industries for the benefit of all Nova Scotians.

INTRODUCTION

Did you know that people have been living in Atlantic Canada for at least twelve thousand years? It's true. And I probably should have given you a spoiler alert, because that's actually Thing Number 3 in this book. Sorry about that.

But, just for a second, pretend that I didn't just give away 1 percent of the book you're holding in your hands. Instead, imagine how many interesting people have walked down your street. Go back in time, before your street was a street, and think about the people who might have hunted or camped on the land your house sits on. Think about how many historic events have happened in your town, and how many times the tiniest seed of an invention took root in the mind of someone living in your province. Add up twelve thousand years' worth of all this, and you'll realize there's a lot you don't know about the place where you live.

This book is packed with interesting stories and facts that were uncovered in a lot of different ways—by reading newspapers, talking to people, doing internet research, visiting the archives, and checking books out of the library. Once you read this book, you'll know one hundred more things about Atlantic Canada—that is, the provinces of New Brunswick, Nova Scotia, Prince Edward Island, and Newfoundland and Labrador—than you knew before, and that's a start. But don't let it end there, because there will still be at least ten thousand more things you don't know.

I hope you read this book, and learn lots of things that amaze and impress your friends, your parents, and your neighbours. But I also hope that when you're done, you start digging up some interesting things of your own. Visit your library. Talk to your grandparents. Read the newspaper. And visit some museums!

Not sure where to start? This book will help with that, too.

Maybe I'll get to read your book someday.

CAMPBELLTON

BATHURST

MIRAMICHI

**NEW
BRUNSWICK**

ATLANTIC

KESWICK

FREDERICTON

NACKAWIC

MONCTON

**PRINCE EDWARD
ISLAND**

SUMMERSIDE

CARDIGAN   **CAPE
BRETO
ISLAN**

CHARLOTTETOWN

ST. STEPHEN   SAINT JOHN

SPRINGHILL

BADDE

PICTOU

BAY OF FUNDY

MIDDLETON

WOLFVILLE

NOVA SCOTIA

ANNAPOLIS
ROYAL   MAHONE BAY   DARTMOUTH

HALIFAX

LUNENBURG

YARMOUTH

SHELBURNE

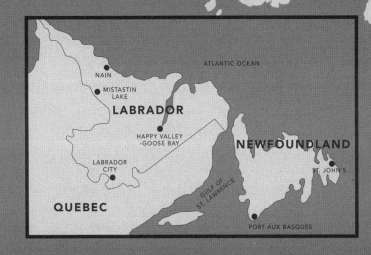

LABRADOR
(SEE INSET)

TWILLINGATE

WESLEYVILLE

CORNER BROOK

GANDER

NEWFOUNDLAND

BONAVISTA

ST. JOHN'S

AN

SYDNEY

LOUISBOURG

ATLANTIC OCEAN

NAIN

MISTASTIN
LAKE

LABRADOR

HAPPY VALLEY
-GOOSE BAY

NEWFOUNDLAND

LABRADOR
CITY

ST. JOHN'S

GULF OF
ST. LAWRENCE

QUEBEC

PORT AUX BASQUES

1

A meteorite hit Labrador about 36 million years ago.

And that meteorite left behind a lot of evidence—in the form of a huge crater. The Mistastin crater in central Labrador used to be about twenty-eight kilometres wide, but it has eroded over time, and now it measures about sixteen kilometres wide. It holds a lot of water, too—the Mistastin crater is also the home of Mistastin Lake. The lake has a small island in the middle of it.

Meteorite craters are amazing things. When a meteorite hits the Earth, it breaks open the Earth's surface, giving us the chance to take a good close look inside our home planet. But sometimes, these craters let us learn about places that are much farther away—like the moon. Recently, Dr. Paul Sylvester from Memorial University's Department of Earth Sciences in Newfoundland worked with a team of scientists to test space technology (like lunar rovers) in the area of the Mistastin crater.

> ### Fun Stuff
> Learn more about space without leaving Newfoundland & Labrador by visiting the Johnson Geo Centre at the base of Signal Hill in St. John's.
> *www.geocentre.ca*

The crater is very similar to a lot of the craters found on the Earth's moon. Since NASA's been busy examining the moon's surface, the Mistastin crater comes in handy—it's the perfect place to practice and test equipment on a moon-like surface right here on Earth before doing the real thing. The Mistastin crater also helps scientists understand more about what happens to a planet when it is hit by a meteor.

2

You can walk on the floor of the Bay of Fundy, which was formed 15 million years ago.

According to the *Guinness Book of World Records*, the world's highest average ocean tides are officially in Minas Basin, Nova Scotia. In the spring, the water rises and falls about 14 metres every day, and that's on average. The very highest tides on record were actually 16.3 metres.

Fun Stuff

From the middle of June until the middle of October, Hopewell Rocks Park is open for exploration. Try to stay for at least four hours so you can see the tide at its highest, and then watch the water empty out. Make sure you save lots of time to walk around on the ocean floor—because that's the best part. *www.thehopewellrocks.ca*

But the Hopewell Rocks in Albert County, New Brunswick, offer a unique way to experience tides that, rising as high as sixteen metres, are often just as high as the ones in Minas Basin. There, you can see "flowerpot rocks" that range between forty and seventy feet tall. The shapes of these huge rocks are really interesting, because the tides don't quite reach all the way to their tops. So when the tide is rushing in and out, twice a day, it's eroding most of the rocks, making them skinnier and skinnier, but because the tops of the rocks are untouched, they flare out. There are also lots of caves.

If you visit the Hopewell Rocks at high tide, you'll see that most of the area is completely under water. But wait four hours and the tide will go out completely, leaving lots of squishy sand, tidepools full of sea life, and interesting rocks, fossils, and shells—the ocean floor is exposed until the tide comes in, which makes it the perfect time to go exploring.

3

The land that makes up Atlantic Canada has been populated for at least 12,000 years.

Canada may have been established in 1867, but people have been living here for much, much, *much* longer than that. In fact, more than five hundred generations of Indigenous people have lived in Atlantic Canada over at least twelve thousand years. That means that Indigenous people have been here about thirty times longer than the Europeans.

The first people who lived in this region include the Innu (Labrador), the Beothuk (Newfoundland), the Mi'kmaq (all of Atlantic Canada), the Wolastoqiyik (New Brunswick), the Inuit (Labrador), and the Passamaquoddy (New Brunswick).

Unfortunately the Beothuk are said to be extinct (but you should read Number 22 and see what you think). Their numbers started dwindling after the Europeans arrived, because of the sudden exposure to European illnesses and a reduction in land (and therefore resources).

The Passamaquoddy are not recognized as First Nations by the Canadian government (the federal government states that the Passamaquoddy in New Brunswick belong to the Passamaquoddy tribe in the US, which they do. But their traditional territory stretched across the Canada-US border, before the Canada-US border existed).

Today, people from all of these Indigenous groups still live in Atlantic Canada (except for the Beothuk, as far as we know. Seriously, go read Number 22).

Learn More

It's important to understand the history of the land you live on. A lot of books on the history of Atlantic Canada only include history from the arrival of the Europeans onward, because Indigenous people preserved their history by telling their stories to younger generations. But oral history is just as important and valuable as written history. Want to learn more? Look for opportunities to hear and read stories by Indigenous people where you live.

4

Around 10,000 years ago, melted glaciers helped form the underground brook that feeds Griffin's Pond in the Halifax Public Gardens.

Nova Scotia was covered in glaciers twenty thousand years ago. But about ten thousand years later, those glaciers melted. When they did, new bodies of water formed all over the province, and Halifax's underwater

Visit the Public Gardens in downtown Halifax and check out Griffin's Pond, a piece of Freshwater Brook that runs above ground.

Freshwater Brook is a perfect example. Just after the glaciers melted, the brook formed in the north part of the Halifax Commons, a giant park in the city's downtown. Except at the time, the brook was above ground.

The brook has been useful throughout history—it supplied water to the British navy and other ships, it fed skating ponds, and supported a brewery on Spring Garden Road.

In the early 1800s, though, Halifax grew quickly. New buildings popped up, more people moved in, and unfortunately, the brook started being used as a sewer. This wasn't unusual for the time—but the practice made the water extremely dirty and unsafe (it certainly couldn't be used for drinking or skating rinks anymore!). And the smell must have been awful. In the end, the brook was buried underground, to allow for more buildings to be built.

If Freshwater Brook ran above ground today, it would flow past Citadel Hill, through the Public Gardens, across Barrington Street, and down into Halifax Harbour. You can still find a little piece of it above ground though—just ask the ducks at Griffin's Pond, in the Public Gardens.

5

The oldest funeral monument in North America is in southern Labrador—and it's 7,500 years old.

In July 1973, a team of archaeologists from Memorial University in Newfoundland set up camp near L'Anse Amour, a tiny village in southern Labrador. Earlier, some archaeologists from Dartmouth College in New Hampshire had found proof that people lived in the area over six thousand years earlier, and the Memorial University scientists wanted to take a closer look. On that trip, they found something interesting, according to an article they published in *Scientific American*. They said it was "a kind of boulder pavement"—basically, it was a layer of rock. They made a note of it, but since they didn't have enough people to focus on that area, they left it alone.

That is until 1974, when they came back with more people and started excavating new areas. One of those sites was the area with the "boulder pavement." After clearing off the pavement, they discovered it was actually the top of a mound of boulders. They kept digging, and almost a metre below the surface of the mound was the almost intact, 7,500-year-old skeleton of a twelve-year-old boy. The boy was a Maritime Archaic Person, part of an ancient group of hunter-gatherers that lived in Labrador thousands of years ago. The mound of boulders was his gravestone.

In the grave, they also found a number of interesting artifacts, including a large walrus tusk, three knives made of quartzite, two graphite pebbles used for painting, a bone tool, a pendant made of bone or antler, and a whistle made of bird bones. The whistle still worked, about 7,500 years later.

Fun Stuff

If you find yourself exploring southern Labrador with your family, visit L'Anse Amour and see this National Historic Site for yourself. While you're there, you can also climb the Point Amour Lighthouse, the tallest lighthouse in Atlantic Canada. *www.newfoundlandlabrador.com*

6

In the 1500s, Acadia was named after an ancient Greek paradise.

In 1523, an Italian explorer named Giovanni da Verrazzano left Dieppe (in France, not New Brunswick!) to explore the Atlantic coast of what is now North America. In his writings, he referred to an area near Delaware as "Archadia," after Greece's Arcadia.

Although Arcadia is an actual region in Greece, it's also a part of Greek mythology. The mythological Arcadia is a beautiful wilderness and the home of Pan, the half-goat, half-human god of the wilderness, shepherds, and hunters. According to legend, Pan spent his time lounging around Arcadia, playing his flute and hanging out with nymphs and dryads.

The name "Arcadia" stuck for a few centuries before evolving into "Acadia." In 1524, around the same time that da Verrazzano was exploring the Atlantic coast, a Portuguese explorer referred to Newfoundland as "Arcadie," and about forty years later, a mapmaker named Bolongnino Zaltieri called the land that is now New Brunswick and Nova Scotia "Larcadia."

Over time, of course, the word evolved, and Archadia, Arcadie, and Larcadia became "Acadie."

Fun Stuff

Since Acadia spans most of Atlantic Canada, there are lots of places you can go to learn more about Acadian culture. In Nova Scotia, visit the Grand Pré National Historic Site and the Acadian Cross. In New Brunswick, visit the Musée Acadien de Caraquet or the Saint-Simon Heritage and Cultural Interpretation Centre. And in Prince Edward Island, there's the Acadian Museum of Prince Edward Island. *www.experiencegrandpre.ca* *www.museecaraquet.ca* *www.museeacadien.org*

7

In 1614, Captain Henry Mainwaring set out to catch a pirate...but became one instead.

If you live in Newfoundland, you've probably heard about Peter Easton, one of the biggest, baddest pirates of the seventeenth century. Easton wasn't always a pirate—he originally went to Newfoundland because England and Spain were at war and Queen Elizabeth I hired him to defend the Newfoundland fishing fleets (which really meant attacking and looting Spanish ships). But when the war ended in 1603 and no one wanted him to attack ships anymore, he just kept doing so anyway. This time, though, he didn't just stick to Spanish ships—he started hanging around the Bristol Channel near England, and took money from British ships that needed to pass through.

Obviously, this didn't go over well, and in 1610, the Earl of Nottingham hired a man named Henry Mainwaring to capture Easton. But by now, Easton had gone back to Newfoundland, where he set up his home base in Harbour Grace—although he did leave whenever he saw a good plundering opportunity.

But instead of doing his job, Mainwaring got distracted and started looting Spanish treasure ships. When he finally arrived in Harbour Grace in 1614, Easton was away capturing treasure ships of his own.

Instead of trying to find Easton, Mainwaring took over the Harbour Grace fort and, with four hundred mariners by his side, started attacking and looting French and Portuguese ships. By the time he sailed back to England, he had £3,400 worth of treasure (which would be over a $1 million today!).

When Mainwaring got back home, King James I (who had taken over for Queen Elizabeth by then) agreed to forgive him for being a pirate, as long as he agreed to stop doing it. Mainwaring agreed, and went on to write a book, become a knight, and fight in the English Civil Wars.

Fun Stuff

If you want to know more about piracy in Newfoundland, visit the Conception Bay Museum in Harbour Grace and check out their Peter Easton exhibit. The museum also features a large aviation exhibit.
www.hgrace.ca

ATLANTIC CANADA

8

In the 1700s, slavery was common in Atlantic Canada (and all over Canada, for that matter).

Many people don't realize that there was slavery in Canada, but there was. Between thirty thousand and forty thousand African Americans were able to escape to Canada from the Southern US via the Underground Railroad, but that was in the early 1800s. Further back, many white Canadians enslaved people too—slavery wasn't abolished in British North America (which included all of the Atlantic provinces) until 1834.

In 1790, for example, between twelve hundred and two thousand Black people were enslaved in New Brunswick, Nova Scotia, and Prince Edward Island. Many people were enslaved in Newfoundland as well. Sometimes governments even used slave-related incentives to get white people to settle in Canada. In 1791, for example, the PEI government passed a law stating that white settlers would receive "forty shillings for every Negro brought by such white person."

And children were enslaved too. Any child born to an enslaved person was automatically considered to be the property of the person who had enslaved their parents. According to a 1777 diary entry written by Simeon Perkins, a Liverpool businessman, he had "purchased" a ten- or eleven-year-old boy named Jacob for just £35. Jacob wasn't even allowed to use his own name—Perkins renamed him Frank.

There are many more stories like this out there. Of course, slavery has been abolished now, but unfortunately, racism still hangs on.

Learn More

This little entry just scratches the surface of the history of Black enslavement in Canada. If you want to learn and understand more about this important topic, visit the Black Cultural Centre of Nova Scotia. *www.web1.bccnsweb.com*

9

People likely started eating pork-less pork pie in Cape Breton sometime in the 1700s.

When someone says the words "pork pie," you probably picture a golden-crusted pie filled with pork. Like a chicken pot pie or a steak pie, but with pork. Unless you're from Cape Breton, that is.

If you *are* from Cape Breton, you know this is all wrong.

The Cape Breton pork pie isn't a pie at all—it's actually a tart. And it's not filled with pork—it's filled with dates, with a bit of orange juice, vanilla, and brown sugar in the mix. The top of the tart is covered in an icing made from maple syrup.

Unfortunately, no one really knows where the name "pork pie" came from, but people are pretty sure the dessert came from Europe. A book called *Pie: A Global History* (can you imagine how much fun the research for that book would have been?) says it is "clearly descended from the medieval European tradition," before going on to say that it was probably either brought over by the French in the early 1700s, or the Scottish in the late 1700s.

Fun stuff

Want to try this amazing dessert? Get an adult on board and you can. Here's the recipe:

Shortbread Shells:
1 cup butter
½ cup icing sugar
1 egg yolk
1 tsp vanilla
2 cups all-purpose flour
2 tbsp cornstarch
¼ tsp salt

Filling:
2 ¼ cups chopped dates
¾ cup brown sugar
¾ cup boiling water
¼ tsp salt
1 tsp vanilla

Icing:
⅔ cup icing sugar
2 tbsp maple syrup
1 tbsp butter, softened

Shells: In a large bowl, cream butter with sugar until fluffy, beat in egg yolk and vanilla. Sift together flour, cornstarch, and salt; gradually stir into creamed mixture, gently kneading until smooth.

Working in batches, gently form dough into 2-cm balls, place in 4-cm tart cups, and press evenly over bottom and sides of cup to form shell. Bake at 325°F for about 18 minutes. Let cool in pan on rack; loosen shells with tip of knife.

Filling: In a small saucepan, bring dates, sugar, water, and salt to a boil over medium heat; reduce heat and simmer, stirring often, for 4 minutes or until thickened and smooth. Let cool; stir in vanilla. Spoon into shells.

Icing: Blend together icing sugar, maple syrup, and butter until smooth; place a dollop onto each tart. Tarts can be stored at room temperature for up to 4 days or frozen for up to 2 weeks.

—The Taste of Nova Scotia Cookbook

10

Canada's first recorded observatory was built at the Fortress of Louisbourg in 1750.

Louisbourg is famous for the significant role it played in the Seven Years' War between France and Great Britain (1756-63). But did you also know that it's the home of Canada's first recorded astronomical observatory?

In 1750, the Marquis de Chabert (Joseph-Bernard Chabert de Cogolin) was well into his mission to make French nautical charts more accurate (nautical charts are kind of like maps for the ocean). By then, he'd already surveyed the shores of Acadia and created charts of Halifax Harbour (then known as the Baie de Chibouctou) and he had just arrived at the Fortress of Louisbourg to observe Île Royale, the island now called Cape Breton.

People have always looked to the stars for navigation. And ocean tides are heavily affected by the gravitational pull between the moon, Earth, and the sun. If Chabert wanted to improve those charts, it was important to understand astronomy. So in 1750, he built a small wooden building with telescopes at the King's Bastion at Louisbourg. From there, he was able to figure out the longitude and latitude of the town of Louisbourg—which was a big deal at the time, because not many people understood how longitude worked yet.

Longitude and latitude are lines that form an imaginary grid over the face of the earth—lines of latitude go across, and lines of longitude go up and down. Each line of latitude has a different number assigned to it, and so does each line of longitude, and together, these numbers are the coordinates. Every place has latitude and longitude coordinates, which work like a special code to find the location.

Fun Stuff

Want to learn more about the stars and planets? Go to one of the Halifax Planetarium's public shows for ages eight and up in the Sir James Dunn building at Dalhousie University. Don't worry, if you're under eight there's an option for you, too—catch a show at Halifax's Discovery Centre instead. *www.astronomynovascotia.ca/index.php/planetarium*

11

In the mid-1700s, people named a Newfoundland island after its terrible smell.

There's a little island about sixty kilometres off the coast of Wesleyville, Newfoundland. It's only 0.8 kilometres by 0.3 kilometres, and nothing really lives there—except *a lot* of birds.

Until the middle of the eighteenth century, the island was called Penguin Island, because thousands and thousands of great auks used to live there—and the great auk looked a lot like a penguin. Unfortunately, the great auk is extinct now, because sailors and settlers started hunting it for its feathers (used for pillows and mattresses). But while the great auks were still living, it seems they spent a lot of their time pooping—all over Penguin Island.

Later in the eighteenth century, the island started showing up on maps with a new name—Funk Island. Most people believe that it was named after the terrible stench of the great auk poop that was all over the island.

This is a vintage drawing of the (unfortunately extinct) great auk. (Can Stock)

And although the great auks are gone now, the poop just keeps piling up—thanks to a huge population of another type of seabird, the thin-billed murre.

Learn More

Do you know how your hometown got its name? Find out by visiting the library, checking the internet, or asking your parents or teachers. There's a story behind almost every place name, and some of those stories are pretty interesting.

12

Crocks Point in New Brunswick was named after an Acadian maple sugar maker who settled there in the 1760s.

Near Keswick, on the east side of the Saint John River, there's a chunk of land called Crocks Point. This piece of land was once an Acadian settlement, and the Cyr family was one of the main families who lived there. This included a man named Jean-Baptiste Cyr II, who settled in the area with his family in the 1760s. That's who the area is named after.

Confused? It will all make sense in a second, because Jean-Baptiste, who was known for making sugar from rock maple, also had a nickname. People called him "Crock." Although we don't know for sure why he was called Crock, there are a few different theories:

- It came from the word *croquer*, which was part of a question he would often ask his customers. The question was "Voulez-vous avoir quelque chose à croquer?" which translates to, "Would you like something to munch on?"
- It was named after his moustache. It was said to have been a *moustache en croc*, a style of moustache that curves up into pointy ends.
- It was named after his weapon of choice, which was reportedly a crochet hook.

Fun Stuff

Want to know how maple candy is made? There are sugar farms you can visit in both Nova Scotia and New Brunswick. Try Sugar Moon Farm and Maplewood Maple Syrup Farm in Nova Scotia or Trites Family Sugar Bush and Dumfries Maples in New Brunswick.

Jean-Baptiste and his family left Crocks Point for Madawaska in 1790, when they (along with the other Acadians in the area) successfully petitioned the British for land in northern New Brunswick.

13

The spelling of Moncton is the result of a mistake made in the 1760s.

Back in 1735, Moncton, New Brunswick, was an Acadian settlement called Le Coude, which, translated to English, means "The Elbow." Now, "The Elbow" probably seems like an odd name for a town, but it was actually pretty appropriate, since the people who named the town were referring to a sharp bend in the Petitcodiac River, which flows through Moncton from the Bay of Fundy.

But twenty years later, Lieutenant Colonel Robert Monckton and his British troops captured the French Fort Beausejour on the Isthmus of Chignecto, which borders New Brunswick and Nova Scotia, renamed it Fort Cumberland, and took over the whole region. Shortly after, the Expulsion of the Acadians began, and the British started forcing Acadians to leave their homes in the Maritime provinces—including Le Coude.

In 1766, a ship arrived from Pennsylvania, carrying eight families of settlers. The family names were Stief, Treitz, Somers, Reicker, Jones, Wortman, Lutz, and Copple. If you live in New Brunswick, you probably know someone with one of those last names (or something similar), because there are lots of descendants still around today.

In any case, when the settlers arrived, they decided to name the town "Monckton," after Lieutenant Colonel Robert Monckton. But when they were filling out the paperwork, a clerk left out the "k," and the town's legal name became "Moncton."

14

Until 1769, Prince Edward Island was part of Nova Scotia.

For a very long time, before Canada was its own country, France and England were fighting over the Atlantic provinces. During that time, they passed bits and pieces of Atlantic Canada back and forth. In the first half of the 1700s, Cape Breton was a French colony called Île Royale. At the time, PEI was called Île Saint-Jean (see Number 18), and was considered part of Île Royale.

In 1756, the Seven Years' War started, but it wasn't really a war on its own, it was just another part of a bigger, ongoing war between France and Britain. Basically, they were fighting for control of the Western world (which included Canada), and both sides had other European countries fighting with them as allies.

When the British captured the Fortress of Louisbourg in Île Royale (Cape Breton) in 1758, they unofficially took all of Île Royale, and with

> ### Fun Stuff
> The Fortress of Louisbourg plays a big part in how all of this happened, and you can still visit it today. Visit *www.novascotia.com* to find out more.

it, Île Saint-Jean (PEI). The Seven Years' War ended in 1763, the two sides signed a treaty, and Britain officially got Île Royale and Île Saint-Jean. So Cape Breton and PEI were both considered part of Nova Scotia until 1769, when PEI appointed a governor and branched out on its own.

15

If a politician named Jonathan Eddy had his way, Nova Scotia would have become part of the US in 1776.

Jonathan Eddy may have been from Massachusetts, but he made all his most embarrassing political moves while living and working in Nova Scotia. He moved to the Chignecto area, near Amherst, in 1763, after serving in the New England military for a few years. He wasn't alone—a lot of people moved to Nova Scotia from Massachusetts around the same time. He became the Deputy Provost Marshal of Cumberland County (this is kind of like a military police officer), and then served as a member of the House of Assembly from 1770 to 1775. Jonathan was kicked out of the House of Assembly on July 20, 1775, because he never showed up to meetings. That's just the boring stuff you need to know—here's where it gets good.

While Jonathan was skipping meetings in Nova Scotia, the American Revolution was kicking into high gear across the border. In case you didn't know, before Canada and the US became independent, both countries were controlled by Britain. Many Americans didn't want to be ruled by Britain anymore, so they fought for their independence—that's what the American Revolution was all about. There were quite a few people who had moved to Nova Scotia from the US at the time, and they were getting a little riled up, too.

In 1776, Jonathan convinced a few of them to form a rebellion—and the goal was to "liberate" Nova Scotia from British rule and make it part of the United States. Their first step was to talk to George Washington about the possibility, but Washington wouldn't help. Then Jonathan and his friends went to the US Congress—but they didn't have any luck there either. Finally, he asked the General Court of Massachusetts for help, and the court told him that if he could gather the people, they'd provide supplies and ammunition.

Fun Stuff

Fort Beausejour-Fort Cumberland is now a National Historic Site, and you can still explore it today. Stop in for a visit and take a selfie dressed as a gate guard, or take part in one of many activities designed just for kids.
www.pc.gc.ca/eng/lhn-nhs/nb/beausejour

After wandering around trying to convince people to help him, Jonathan ended up gathering about eighty people. He brought that number up to one hundred and eighty by threatening to destroy people's homes if they didn't join him.

On November 12, 1776, Jonathan and his army tried to attack Fort Cumberland, but the fort commander was ready for him, and the attack failed. Then they tried to attack the fort again—this time lighting buildings on fire. Again, someone warned the British. They tried to put together a third attack but this time an English warship with four hundred men showed up. That ended Jonathan's efforts to "liberate" Nova Scotia. He escaped with his men to Maine, and lived in the US for the rest of his life.

16

On July 1, 1782, a woman named Sylvia helped protect the town of Lunenburg.

American privateers (people who were hired by governments to raid enemy ships) raided Lunenburg, Nova Scotia, in the summer of 1782. On July 1, a few ships landed nearby, and about 170 American privateers poured into the small town, even taking prisoners. One of those prisoners was Colonel John Creighton, who was held for ransom and whose house was

This painting, called The Sack of Lunenburg, *is how artist A. L. Wright imagined the attack on Lunenburg by American privateers in 1782. (Nova Scotia Archives)*

burned down. But the hero of this story is one of Creighton's servants, a Black woman known only as Sylvia, who cared for Creighton's house and children.

When the raid began, Creighton went to a blockhouse nearby to try and stop it. Sylvia followed behind, with gun cartridges and musket balls hidden in her apron, and when she got there she helped load muskets for the militia. When the blockhouse was taken, Sylvia escaped and went back to the house, where she saved Creighton's son, Joseph, by throwing her body over his to protect him from enemy bullets. Then, she collected all of the family's valuables, put them in a chest, and sat on it, hiding the chest under her skirt.

When the soldiers tried to raid the house, she pretended to be scared of them, and they more or less ignored her while they raided the rest of the house (which didn't have anything of any value left, because Sylvia had hidden it all it the chest). When the privateers gave up and left, Sylvia hid the chest in the well, saving it from the fire that would destroy the house.

Fun Stuff

Sylvia had to be incredibly brave to do everything that she did. Who is the bravest person you know and what makes them brave? Write a short story or draw a comic about that person and their brave actions, and give it to them as a gift.

17

A 13-year-old boy rescued people from a shipwreck in 1797.

On the afternoon of November 23, 1797, a frigate (which is a type of warship) called the HMS *Tribune* ran into serious trouble near Halifax. The frigate's captain had decided they didn't need a local pilot to help them navigate the ship safely into port. As a result, the ship moved off-course and hit Thrumcap Shoal, an area of shallow water in the Halifax Harbour.

The crew called for help, but because of the high winds, only one rescue boat made it—which wasn't much help, since there were about 250 passengers and crewmembers on board.

When the tide started to rise, the ship floated up and off the shoal, but the crew soon discovered damage and the ship started to sink. To make matters worse, it was still incredibly windy and the wind damaged the rudder, which helps steer the boat. The sinking ship floated across the harbour and crashed into the rocks along Herring Cove, close to where Tribune Head is today.

A few officers got to land, but most of the passengers had to try and survive the night by holding onto the ship's rigging. That night, most of the passengers died. But in the morning, two were saved by the first person to reach the ship after it landed in Herring Cove—a thirteen-year-old boy known only as Joe Cracker. Between ten and twelve more people were saved by other rescue boats after that.

Today, we don't even know Joe Cracker's real name. But he's remembered by a memorial on Tribune Head that reads: "In memory of the heroism of Joe Cracker, the fisher lad of 13 years who was the first to rescue survivors from the wreck of HMS *Tribune* in a heavy sea off this headland 24th November 1797."

Fun Stuff

If you have an adventurous spirit and an adult to go along with you, you could see where the wreck happened—and visit the memorial plaque for yourself. You'll just need to do a little hiking up Tribune Head. But watch your step—the trail might be overgrown. 44°34'00"N, 63°33'19"W

18

Until 1799, Prince Edward Island was called the Island of St. John.

When the Acadian people began settling on what is now known as Prince Edward Island around 1720, they decided to call it Île Saint-Jean. Of course, when they arrived, the Island already had a name—Epekwitk, which means "resting on the waves." This is the name the Mi'kmaq people gave the Island, and it's based on a legend about how Kluscap spent years sleeping on its shores. According to Mi'kmaw oral tradition, Kluscap was the first man to be created and brought to life by the Great Spirit. Kluscap plays a major role in a lot of Wabanaki stories (the Wabanaki Confederacy is a group that includes the Mi'kmaq, Maliseet, Passamaquoddy, Abenaki, and Penobscot).

But the Acadians gave it another name, and that name stuck for a long time—shifting to the Island of St. John or St. John's Island when the Seven Years' War ended and the British officially took over in 1763.

It remained St. John's Island until 1799, when the British decided to rename it (again!). After considering other names, including "New Ireland," they settled on "Prince Edward Island" because they wanted to name it after the Duke of Kent, who led the British forces in North America during the war (and whose real name, of course, was Prince Edward).

Fun Stuff

Europeans first settled on Prince Edward Island about 300 years ago. But the Island has been home to the Mi'kmaq people for much longer. Visit the Lennox Island Mi'kmaq Cultural Centre and learn about what life on Prince Edward Island was like for thousands of years. *www.lennoxisland.com/ attractions/cultural-centre*

19

Nalujuk Night, which probably began in the 1800s, is a spooky—but fun—night for children in northern Labrador's Inuit communities.

In the northern part of Labrador, January 6 is a special night full of fear and fun—particularly in Inuit communities like Nain and Makkovik. In these areas, January 6 is Nalujuk Night, a Christmas tradition that marks the end of the holidays. According to legend, creatures called Nalujuit travel across the ice from Greenland to these northern communities. Generally the Nalujuit are dressed in furs and skins, and wearing scary-looking white masks.

When they arrive, the Nalujuit chase the children, threatening to hit them with the weapons they carry—usually sticks or harpoons. Luckily, if the children are caught, they can protect themselves by singing a song. In some cases, Nalujuit give treats to the children they catch (after the children sing, of course).

Sometimes Nalujuit go into the children's houses with gifts, and in some houses, children hang stockings for the Nalujuit to fill on Nalujuk Night. If a Nalujuit visits, the children have to sing a song for them before the creature will leave.

Of course, these Nalujuit are actually adults and teenagers dressed up in costumes. And although the tradition can make for a pretty scary evening, it's also a lot of fun.

Fun Stuff

This fall, ask an older family member about the holiday traditions they liked best when they were a kid. Pick one and add a new tradition to your favourite winter holiday celebration.

20

In the early 1800s, pirate treasure was buried near Quidi Vidi Lake in St. John's, Newfoundland.

In his book *Ghosts and Oddities*, Jack Fitzgerald tells a story of treasure that takes place about two hundred years ago, when the British Navy was chasing a group of pirates. They didn't want the navy to get ahold of their treasure (which was worth about $75,000 at the time), so they buried it near Quidi Vidi Lake. Twenty years later, one of those pirates came back to get it but, unfortunately for him, got sick and died before he could go dig it up.

But the pirate's bad luck was a St. John's man's good fortune. When he died, the pirate had been staying with a man with the last name O'Regan. The book says he ran a shoe store. O'Regan treated the pirate well, so when the pirate died, he gave O'Regan the treasure map.

Once the pirate was dead, O'Regan went looking for the treasure. The story says that, with the help of some local fishermen, he found the treasure, and moved to the United States. But he didn't take all of the treasure with him, which meant there should still be some left buried back in Newfoundland.

Another book, Edward Butts's *Ghost Stories of Newfoundland and Labrador*, mentions this same area, writing that the notorious pirate Captain William Kidd buried five kegs of gold there. Although this could be the same treasure Fitzgerald was writing about, it's possible there was even more treasure in the same place.

Regardless, people did search for the rest of the treasure, but if anyone ever found it, they never told anyone else.

Fun Stuff

Want to find a small treasure of your own? Try geocaching, a real-life treasure-hunting activity where people hide small objects for others to find. Get a parent or other adult to help you find a geocaching website that's based in your area. As long as you've got an adult and GPS, you're ready to go treasure hunting.

21

In the mid-1800s, Rose Fortune became the first female police officer in Canada.

Rose Fortune was about ten years old in 1783, when she moved to Annapolis Royal with her parents. We don't know much about her childhood,

We don't know who painted this watercolour portrait of Rose, but it may have been done sometime during the 1830s. (Nova Scotia Archives)

but based on the documentation that's been found, we do know that she came from Philadelphia. Since she arrived in Annapolis Royal at the end of the American Revolution, it's assumed that her parents were Black Loyalists—Black Americans who fought for the British during the American Revolution in exchange for their freedom. (Note: the British often didn't make good on this promise, but that's a whole separate story.)

In her older years, though, Rose was pretty well known around Annapolis Royal. She built her own business as a delivery person, using a wheelbarrow to carry visitors' luggage from the wharf to their hotel and back again. She started a wake-up-call service for travellers, and she also took care of the docks—protecting property, and setting up (and enforcing) curfews. That's how she became known as Canada's first unofficial policewoman.

She ran a pretty tight ship, too. According to multiple sources, a Lieutenant-Colonel Sleigh of the 77th Regiment hired her to carry his bags in 1852. He wrote about the experience later, saying, "She had a small stick in her hand which she applied lustily to the backs of all who did not jump instantly out of the way."

Rose died in Fort Anne on February 20, 1864, and she's buried in the Royal Garrison Cemetery. But her family—and her legacy—lives on. She has a long list of descendants, including Annapolis Royal mayor Daurene Lewis, who was also the first Black Canadian woman to become a mayor. The Association of Black Law Enforcers also offers a scholarship in Rose's name.

Fun Stuff

Curious about the area where Rose lived and worked? Check out the Fort Anne National Historic Site to try on some historic clothing, go on a ghost tour, or visit the Garrison Cemetery.
www.pc.gc.ca/en/lhn-nhs/ns/fortanne

22

Some people believe that Shawnadithit, who died in 1829, was not the last Beothuk.

The Beothuk are the Indigenous people of Newfoundland and Labrador. Around 1497, when the Europeans arrived, there were between five hundred and one thousand Beothuk, mainly living on the south and northeast coasts of the province. But they moved inland—away from the areas where they fished—when the Europeans started building significant settlements along the coast. As Europeans built more and more settlements, the Beothuk got pushed out again, this time by the fur traders who were hunting in the area.

At this point, the Beothuk were far away from the territory they'd known for centuries. This made survival difficult, especially since (according to some historians) they'd also been exposed to tuberculosis from the Europeans. By the 1800s, there were hardly any Beothuk left. The last known living Beothuk, a woman named Shawnadithit, died in 1829.

> ### Learn More
> Visit the Beothuk Interpretation Centre in Boyd's Cove, Newfoundland and Labrador, and see the remains of the Beothuk village site discovered by archaeologists in the 1980s. *www.seethesites.ca/the-sites/ beothuk-interpretation-centre*

However, according to Mi'kmaw oral tradition, the Beothuk never became extinct—they simply integrated with other Indigenous groups on the mainland. According to Mi'sel Joe, the chief of Miawpukek First Nation (quoted in a 2013 article in Labrador City's *Aurora* newpaper), DNA testing has already proven that the Beothuk and Mi'kmaq are connected.

In 2017, an American woman named Carol Reynolds Boyce came forward with the results of a genetics test performed by a company called Accu-Metrics. The results show that she has Beothuk genes, but scientists argue there simply isn't enough Beothuk genetic information available to say for sure.

23

In 1836, 35 children came by boat to work in New Brunswick.

These days, most kids don't get their first jobs until they're around sixteen years old. Some kids work earlier, of course—babysitting, mowing lawns, or shovelling snow—but these are usually just ways to earn a little spending money.

During the Victorian era (1837–1901) in London, England, life was very different. Children from wealthy families didn't work, but children from poor families did. They'd work in mines, factories, and other dangerous places, and they'd sometimes start when they were just four or five years old.

There were also a lot of children living in the streets, a mix of orphans and runaways. A lot of them had to steal to survive, but some of them had jobs too.

In the early 1830s, a group called the Children's Friend Society decided to start sending these street children to work in other places. Thirty-five of those children (thirty-four boys and one girl) left London on a ship called the *Hinde*, and arrived in Newfoundland on June 2, 1836. Then, they had to get on another small boat called a steamer. They landed in Frederiction, New Brunswick, on June 4, 1836, and were sent out to the village of Stanley, New Brunswick, where they were to work as apprentices (workers who practice doing a new job by working with more experienced people). It's hard to know exactly what work the children did when they arrived, but a few were apprenticed to a carpenter in the area.

Some of these children seemed to do well in this new environment, but many of them weren't even living in Stanley anymore by 1851, which means that they probably didn't find permanent homes and had to go somewhere else.

> ### Learn More
> If it's between June 1 and October 15, why not take a road trip to the Central New Brunswick Woodmen's Museum in Boisetown, New Brunswick? Check out the sawmill, the machine sheds, and the blacksmith's shop, and get an idea of the kind of work Victorian kids did every day.
> *www.woodmensmuseum.com*

PRINCE EDWARD ISLAND

24

In 1853, a mysterious incident occurred in Charlottetown when a boat sank near Pictou.

Canada Post commemorated this spooky story with a special stamp, so there's a good chance that if you live in Charlottetown, you know this already. But the story is just too good to leave out.

In the mid-1800s, government mail was delivered by ship. The *Fairy Queen*, a steamer that carried mail and passengers, travelled a regular route between Charlottetown, Prince Edward Island, and Pictou, Nova Scotia. Until October 7, 1853, that is.

One day earlier, the ship left Charlottetown with thirteen passengers and thirteen crew-members. The trip went relatively well at first, but as the ship travelled farther down the Northumberland Strait, the wind picked up and the waves started sloshing over the sides. Despite the terrible conditions, they kept going—until about five hours later, when the ship's steering rope broke.

Although the crew eventually managed to fix it, the storm and the lost steering rope had caused the boat to get a little out of control. Waves started coming up over the side of the ship again—but this time they reached far enough to put out the boiler fires. These generated the steam that kept the boat moving. Without steam, the ship couldn't go anywhere. The water kept rising, and the ship started to sink. It wasn't long before it capsized completely.

Some people got away on a lifeboat, and nine people survived by holding onto pieces of the ship until they could be rescued. At around midnight on October 7, seven people died—two men, a boy, and four women. This is where the facts end and legend begins.

Fun Stuff

These days, most people don't send letters very often, but collecting stamps can be a fun way to learn about people, places, and events. Buy a scrapbook and start collecting! Don't get mail? No problem—just ask your parents and other relatives to start saving them for you. (And keep an eye out for those Haunted Canada stamps!)

In Charlottetown, something strange happened around midnight that same night. A sea captain heard a bell ringing downtown. Since it seemed odd for a bell to ring in the middle of the night, he went over to a nearby church, Kirk of St. James, where the sound seemed to be coming from. When he looked inside, he saw three women, dressed in long white robes, ringing the bell in the bell tower. They didn't seem to notice him. Even more mysteriously, the doors to the tower were locked.

Later, the whole incident was blamed on the wind. But it's interesting that three of the women who died when the *Fairy Queen* sank were regular attendees at the Kirk of St. James church.

CANADA

PHANTOM BELL RINGERS / LES SONNEUSES FANTÔMES, PE

This stamp was released by Canada Post in 2016 as part of their Haunted Canada series. See if you can collect any of these spooky souvenirs! (© 2016 Canada Post)

25

Gold was first discovered in Nova Scotia in 1858.

Did you know that Nova Scotia had its own Gold Rush? In fact, it actually had three! Records say a British army officer named Captain Champagne L'Estrange was the first to discover and document Nova Scotia gold, way back in 1858, while hunting in Mooseland, which is in Musquodoboit Valley.

A couple of years after that, in 1860, a man named John Gerrish Pulsifer found more gold in the same area. Three Mi'kmaw guides named Joe Paul, Noel Louis, and Frank Cope deserve a bunch of the credit, though—these three men were with both L'Estrange *and* Pulsifer when the discoveries were made. This time, the gold was registered with the province.

Before long, people were coming from all over to search for gold in Nova Scotia—in 1871, there were 568 gold miners in the province. A second gold rush lasted from 1896 to 1903, and a third went from 1932 to 1942. All three gold rushes combined, they found 861,105.30 troy ounces—which equals almost 27 tons.

There was gold all over the province—Cape Breton, Wine Harbour, Harrigan Cove, Tangier, Mount Uniacke, the Ovens, West Caledonia, and Kemptville, just to name a few places. It's no wonder so many people came to try their hand at gold digging!

Learn More

If you're wondering if you had gold in your area, there's a cool map that has all the answers. Click on different parts of the interactive map, and learn interesting facts about all the gold districts in Nova Scotia. Go to *www.novascotiagold.ca*, then click on Explore by Theme > Gold Mining > Discovery > Gold Map.

26

The provincial fossil of Nova Scotia was found in Joggins in 1859.

And it just happens to be the only fossil of the world's oldest known reptile, the *Hylonomus lyelli*—and the first known evolutionary link between sea creatures and their development into land-based animals.

The man who discovered it, Sir John William Dawson, was born in Pictou, Nova Scotia, in 1820 and went on to attend Pictou Academy, where he learned a lot about Latin, Greek, Hebrew, physics, and biology. But his knowledge of geology and natural history was mostly self-taught. When he was young (probably in his teens) he would wander the area searching for rocks and shells.

As an adult, he turned his hobby into a profession, and became a highly respected geologist and paleontologist (among other things). One of his great accomplishments was the discovery of the *Hylonomus lyelli*, which he found in the stump of a fossilized tree in Joggins in 1859. Dawson named the fossil after his friend and mentor, geologist Sir Charles Lyell.

The fossil is believed to be 312 million years old, and belongs to what was once a twenty-centimetre-long amphibian that survived mainly on millipedes and other insects. It's now housed at the Natural History Museum in London, England.

Fun Stuff

If you want to know more about fossils, you should go explore the area where the *Hylonomus lyelli* was originally discovered. Joggins Fossil Cliffs offers guided tours ranging from thirty minutes to four hours. Find out more at *www.jogginsfossilcliffs.net*.

27

In 1860, a New Brunswick postmaster general put his own face on a stamp.

Charles Connell held a lot of jobs in his lifetime—over the years, he was a lumberman, a politician, and a businessman. But it wasn't until 1860, two years after he became New Brunswick's postmaster general, that he really left his mark.

In 1859, Connell ordered some new New Brunswick postage stamps from a company in New York. The public had no idea what they'd look like—they only found out when the shipment was received (sometime in early 1860). And based on the news reports, people were pretty surprised. The one-cent stamp had a picture of a wood-burning train, the ten-cent stamp featured Queen Victoria, the twelve-and-a-half-cent stamp had a paddle steamer (a kind of ship), and the seventeen-cent stamp featured the Prince of Wales, who was planning to visit the area later that year.

But it was the five-cent stamp, which featured a portrait of Charles Connell himself, that really got people upset. A lot of people considered Connell's decision to put his own face on a postage stamp to be conceited and inappropriate. The government allowed all stamps except for the five-cent stamp to be circulated right away; the five-cent stamp had to be reprinted with the Queen's portrait instead.

Connell resigned from his job about a week later. Around the same time, he also bought most of the five-cent stamps and burned them on his lawn. He didn't get them all, though. There are still a few around, and they're worth a lot more than five cents. According to *Canadian Stamp News*, this stamp is now worth $36,000.

Fun Stuff

Want to know more about this dramatic moment in history? You're in luck—you can visit Connell's house, which is now a National Historic Site on 128 Connell Street in Woodstock, New Brunswick.

28

The sea mink was hunted to extinction in 1860.

Minks are mammals with long, thin bodies, soft fur, and pointy snouts. Because they're nocturnal you probably won't ever see one, but if you do, you might mistake it for a weasel or a ferret. Today, there are two species of minks—the European mink and the American mink—but until about 1860, there was a third species: the sea mink (*Neovison macrodon*). It lived in rocky parts of the Atlantic coast, mainly in New Brunswick and Newfoundland. It was about twice the size of the American mink, which is usually around eighteen inches long. Its fur was red, it spent most of its time swimming, and it mainly ate fish and mollusks.

And that's pretty much all we know, because the species completely disappeared around 1860. Although fur isn't as popular now as it was then, Canada still has a strong fur trade (which means we sell a lot of fur to places, specifically Europe, Asia, and the United States). Mink fur has always been highly valued for its softness and its shine and, unfortunately, so many people hunted the sea mink in the 1800s that it went extinct. It happened so fast that scientists didn't even have time to develop a scientific description of the species before it was all gone.

> ### Fun Stuff
> Want to know what kinds of wild animals live near you? Find a trail near your house and go for a nature walk. Bring a notebook, walk quietly, and keep an eye out for wildlife—then write down a description of anything that interests you.

29

In 1862, a 16-year-old Nova Scotia girl went to work for P. T. Barnum.

When Anna Swan was born in 1846, she weighed eighteen pounds—about ten pounds more than the average newborn baby. She spent the first part of her childhood living with her parents in Millbrook, Nova Scotia, doing usual kid stuff like playing in the yard, reading, and helping her parents out around the house. But as Anna got older, she continued to grow faster than kids usually do—by the time she was four, she was four foot six inches. Her mother was five foot three inches, so that means that when Anna was four, the top of her head probably reached higher than her mother's shoulders.

Even though people tried to help her out, school must have been a little tough for Anna, since she was too big for the desks the other kids sat in. When she was fifteen, she moved to Truro to live with her aunt and attend the Teacher's College (at the time, it was called the Provincial Normal School, which is kind of weird). But people treated her differently in Truro because of her height, so she moved back home.

When she was sixteen, P. T. Barnum of Barnum & Bailey Circus asked her if she would be a part of an exhibit at his American Museum in New York. At this point, she was seven feet, eleven inches tall and weighed about four hundred pounds. He offered her $1,000 a month (which was a lot at the time) and told her he'd provide her with a tutor three hours a day for three years. Since this was her chance to get more education, Anna agreed to go, and spent her days wearing a dress made of 150 yards of material, and chatting with the thousands of people who visited her at the museum. After a while, she was allowed to participate in singing and theatre performances, and eventually she started touring Europe.

Fun Stuff

Some of Anna's things can still be found at the Tatamagouche Creamery Square. Visit the Margaret Fawcett Norrie Heritage Centre to learn more about Anna's life (plus see her wedding dress, which was given to her by Queen Victoria). *www.creamerysquare.ca*

She eventually married a man from Kentucky named Captain Martin Van Buren Bates. He was very tall, too—seven feet, two inches. When they married, they moved to Ohio, bought a farm, and built a huge house designed to make them both feel comfortable. The house had fourteen-foot ceilings and extra-large furniture.

You've probably heard of P. T. Barnum and his circus. This advertisement from the Acadia Recorder *says that the circus was travelling to Halifax, Nova Scotia, in 1876. (Nova Scotia Archives)*

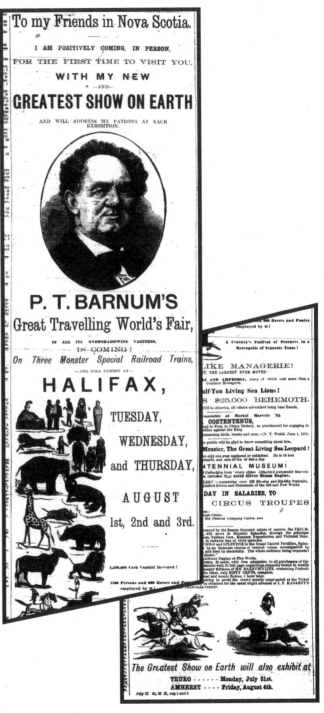

Here is Anna Swan in her wedding dress, given to her as a gift by Queen Victoria. (Nimbus Publishing)

30

In 1863, a logging town named Scotia was founded in California.

Originally, though, it was called Forestville. A company called Pacific Lumber founded the northern California town after buying six thousand acres of forest for just $1.25 an acre.

By 1888, the company had about three hundred employees, and there were a lot of Maritimers living in the area. They were mainly from New Brunswick and Nova Scotia, who (this is just an educated guess because of the timing and the location) likely left Canada's east coast for the US during the California Gold Rush.

The company and the town both got bigger and bigger, until the town was finally big enough to have its own post office. But when it was discovered that there was already a Forestville nearby, they had to change their name (otherwise their mail might go to the wrong Forestville). They decided to rename the town either "Scotia" or "Brunswick" and, according to local California legend, they settled on Scotia after tossing a coin. The name was officially changed on July 9, 1888, and the town called Scotia, California, still exists.

Learn More

While logging is historically an important industry in New Brunswick, we have to make sure that we protect a lot more forest than we cut. Different environments need more protection than others. Turning land into a park can be one way to protect it. New Brunswick's first provincial park was established in Glenwood in 1935. If you're ever driving along Route 17, near Restigouche, New Brunswick, keep an eye out!

31

In the late 1800s, boys as young as 11 worked in Nova Scotia mines.

They were called colliery boys, and there were a lot of them. In 1874, there were 3,939 working miners in Nova Scotia, and 555 were boys under the age of eighteen. In 1890, the number of colliery boys had jumped to 1,102 of 5,119 working miners.

Colliery boys were given a couple of different jobs to do. Usually, they worked as "trappers," which meant sitting alone in the dark most of the time. Their job was to open and shut the doors between the mine shafts so that horses and miners could pass through. Sometimes they worked as "cage runners," bringing boxes full of coal out of the shafts and taking empty boxes back in. They also ran errands, like delivering supplies and cleaning lamps.

Colliery boys were paid less than the older miners, too. In 1880, the pay for adult miners was between 80¢ and $1.50 per day, but boys only got about 65¢ per day. Of course, this was dangerous work, and sometimes the boys were badly injured or killed in mining accidents—the Springhill mining disaster in 1891 killed seventeen boys under the age of seventeen.

Over time, though, the provincial government raised the minimum age for miners. In 1891, they changed the law so that boys between the ages of twelve and sixteen couldn't work in the mines unless they had already finished seventh grade. As times changed, the number of colliery boys dropped. By 1914, only 831 out of 13,632 miners were colliery boys.

> **Fun Stuff**
>
> Wondering what it might have been like to be a colliery boy? Take a tour of the Miners' Museum in Cape Breton and find out. *www.minersmuseum.com/ experience-the-museum*

32

In 1875, Grace Annie Lockhart became the first Canadian woman to graduate with a university degree.

Childhood couldn't have been easy for Grace Annie. She was born in Saint John, New Brunswick, on February 22, 1855, and her mother died just nine months later. According to an archivist at Mount Allison University in Sackville, Annie had three older sisters and a father, who was Grace Annie's official guardian, but he probably spent most of his time at work. She was raised by the family's housekeeper, Rosanna Wilson. Unfortunately Rosanna died too, when Grace Annie was only eight years old.

Luckily, the Lockhart sisters had inherited a bit of money from their grandfather, which they were able to use to pay for school. All four girls went to Mount Allison College (now Mount Allison University) but only Grace Annie stayed for longer than a year. In 1874, she earned a Mistress of Liberal Arts. (At the time, some programs had gender-specific names. Weird, huh?) The following year, she earned a Bachelor of Science, making her the first Canadian woman to earn a university degree—and making Mount Allison College the first school to grant a degree to a woman.

Learn More

Imagine what it must have been like growing up in a time when even some of the degrees had special names for women. How would you feel about that? Why would you feel that way?

Here is Grace Annie from the class of 1875, when she was a student at Mount Allison Wesleyan College. (Mount Allison University Archives, 2007.07/334)

NOVA SCOTIA

33

In 1888, Halifax built a pond in the Halifax Commons, where the skateboard park is now.

If you go to the Halifax Commons now, you'll find a wading pool, a playground, The Pavilion (an all-ages music club), a whole lot of green space, and a skate park. Although people started skateboarding in the 1940s or '50s, the sport didn't really explode until the 1990s. When it did, a group of people formed the Halifax Skate Park Coalition, with the goal of building a skate park in Halifax. In 1995, they did just that.

But before the skate park was there, there was a small body of water called

This photo was taken in 1918, on the Halifax Commons near Egg Pond. (Nova Scotia Archives)

Egg Pond, which was built in 1888. In the summer, people would go there to swim and punt ("punting" is pushing yourself around in a boat using a long pole), and in the winter the pond was used as a skating rink. The changing rooms were in the building that now houses The Pavilion.

There was a playground on the Commons in the early 1900s, too. It was mostly made up of swing sets and piles of sand for kids to play in.

Fun Stuff

Wish you could still skate on Egg Pond? If skateboarding and BMXing isn't your thing, the Oval skating rink is right next-door on the Halifax North Common. Best of all, the fun doesn't stop with winter—just pull on your inline skates, strap on your helmet, and go! Find out more at *www.halifax.ca/recreation/facilities-fields/emera-oval*.

34

In the 1890s, a brave father saved his remarkable daughter from death—by amputating part of her legs.

Kirkina Mucko (Mukko) was born in Labrador in the 1890s, near the remote Inuit community of Rigolet (the community's Inuit name is Kikiaq). When she was just two years old, something happened to her mother. It's an old story, which sometimes makes it hard to find out what happened exactly, but some people say the mother was giving birth, and others say she was seriously ill. No matter which version is true, Kirkina's father had to rush out in the middle of a huge winter storm to get help from Rigolet. Because of the weather it took him a long time to get back home, and by the time he did, Kirkina's mother had passed away and Kirkina's legs were so frostbitten they had turned black.

Kirkina's father knew that his daughter would die if he didn't do something quickly. So he did something incredibly brave—he amputated the bottom half of both of her legs with an axe. He stopped the bleeding somehow (there are different stories about this part, too) and Kirkina survived to live a long, healthy life (she only passed away in 1970). Sometimes she used prosthetic legs, and other times she moved around on her knees, using leather pads to protect them.

She eventually married and had seven children, but her family died from influenza in 1918. After that, she decided to become a nurse and midwife, and she spent the rest of her life helping others in the Rigolet area and later in Happy Valley-Goose Bay. There is now a women's shelter in Rigolet called Kirkina House, named after her.

Learn More

If you live near Rigolet, or your family decides to visit someday, try to imagine what it must have been like for Kirkina as she grew up there. And don't miss the boardwalk—it's the second-longest one in the world.

35

The first Canadian book to sell more than 1 million copies was written by a Nova Scotian and published in 1894.

Have you ever read *Beautiful Joe*? If not, you should give it a try. It's a classic Canadian middle-grade book (that means it's for people who are close to your age) about a dog who was abused by his owner, and then rescued and cared for by a new family. This book is a big deal for a few reasons: it's written from the perspective of the dog (Beautiful Joe); it was inspired in part by another very famous book (*Black Beauty*); it raised awareness of animal cruelty at a time when most people didn't really think about things like that; and it was the first Canadian book to sell more than 1 million copies.

The author of the book is Margaret Marshall Saunders, who was born in Milton, Nova Scotia, and then spent part of her childhood in Berwick before moving to Halifax with her family. She attended schools in Scotland and France, and later she travelled a lot. *Beautiful Joe* was inspired by a dog Margaret met while travelling with her brother to Ontario.

Margaret had published a few things before *Beautiful Joe*, including a short story and a romance novel. She heard about an American Humane Education Society Prize Competition called "Kind and Cruel Treatment of Domestic Animals and Birds in the Northern States" just after the romance novel was published. *Beautiful Joe* was a perfect fit, so she changed the book's setting to Maine (to make it eligible for the US contest) and entered. When it won, Margaret received a $200 prize and, in 1894, the book was published.

It was incredibly popular. Once it was published, it only took six years to sell 625,000 copies in the US, 146,000 copies in the UK, and 558,000 copies in Canada. By the late 1930s, it had sold more than 7 million copies.

Fun Stuff

It's tricky to tell a story from an animal's point of view, but that's exactly what Margaret did—and she did it really well. Why not try it for yourself? Choose a wild or domesticated animal and write a short story that shows what life is like for that animal.

36

The first lollipops were made in St. Stephen, New Brunswick, in 1895.

In St. Stephen, New Brunswick, there's a candy-making company with a long, inventive history. When two brothers, James and Gilbert Ganong, first founded Ganong Brothers Ltd. in 1873, their company mainly sold groceries, but before long, Gilbert noticed they were making most of their money by selling cakes, oysters, and—you guessed it—candy.

At first, the candy they sold came from Saint John, and then the US, but eventually they started making their own, and that's when things really took off. In 1885, one of their candy makers invented Chicken Bones, hard pink cinnamon candies with chocolate in the middle. Four years later, they installed a candy-making machine that could make thousands of hard candies every day. And in 1895, Ganong started making All-Day Suckers. They were available in a bunch of flavours, including orange, strawberry, peppermint, and licorice, and instead of the papery sticks we have today, the candy had wooden butchers' skewers in the middle of them.

Fun Stuff

Want to see Ganong Brothers in action? Visit The Chocolate Museum in St. Stephen and explore the original Ganong factory, check out candy exhibits, and find out how chocolates are made. Find out more at *www.chocolatemuseum.ca*.

But of course, Ganong Brothers didn't stop there. They made the first chocolate nut bar in North America in 1910, and became the first Canadian candy maker to sell chocolates in heart-shaped boxes, in 1930.

37

Harry Houdini escaped from a cell in Halifax City Hall in 1896.

By the time he died on October 31, 1926, entertainer Harry Houdini had become famous for his incredible feats of escape. He escaped from jail cells, straitjackets, milk cans filled with water, and a box that had been bound with rope and dropped into the East River in New York. He even had an act where he'd swallow more than fifty needles.

But he wasn't always a success. Before he was an escape artist, he was a magician—and not a very popular one. It was during this time in his life, when he needed work and money, that he and his wife (who was also his assistant) agreed to tour the Maritimes with the Marco Magic Company.

It didn't go well. In Halifax, one of his publicity stunts involved attempting to escape from ropes that tied him to the back of a horse—but the horse was a little too wild, and took off running onto the road with Houdini on its back. Houdini did escape, but no one was around to see it—he and the horse were too far away by then. There were also problems with the Marco Magic Company—it didn't have a good reputation at all. When the company started having financial troubles, it took off and left Houdini and his wife behind. Since they had no money, they ended up sleeping in the hallway of a hotel.

But that didn't stop Houdini from performing, and one of those performances took place in Halifax City Hall. The feat he performed there was an early version of the one he would perform in Europe a few years later. The police locked his clothes in a cell (all except for a bathing suit). Then they handcuffed him and left him locked up in a separate cell in the basement of City Hall. He escaped, and two hotel clerks noticed him wandering the streets in his bathing suit not long after—before the police even realized he'd left his cell!

Learn More

Harry Houdini did a lot of really interesting things. Next time you go to the library, ask the librarian for help finding a book or video that might tell you more about him.

38

In 1905, Alexander Graham Bell invented a kite that could lift a person.

Alexander Graham Bell never took time off from having ideas. In fact, he hadn't even finished inventing the telephone when he decided to try creating something else amazing: a flying machine.

In the mid-1890s, he started doing kite experiments in the Cape Breton Island town of Baddeck, Nova Scotia, and the whole town got in on the act. People would hang around nearby to watch, take pictures, or help out. And

Alexander Graham Bell and his wife, Mabel Hubbard Gardiner Bell, who is standing inside one of his tetrahedral kites. (Gilbert H. Grosvenor Collection of Photographs of the Alexander Graham Bell Family, Library of Congress)

picture this: because he wanted his invention to be able to carry a person, the kites were so large that he used horses to try and get them into the air. He'd tie a rope from the kite to a horse and then send the horse running across the fields.

This went on for a long time without much success. He tried a lot of different shapes and structures, but nothing worked—until Bell invented the tetrahedral kite in the early 1900s, which was a big step in the right direction. A tetrahedron is a shape made up of four equilateral triangles, in case you were wondering.

After that, Bell focused his experiments on different types of tetrahedral kites, and in 1905, he finally reached his goal. On December 28, one of his kites lifted a man named Neil MacDermid thirty feet into the air.

On December 6, 1907, he took the whole thing a step farther with an even bigger tetrahedral kite called the Cygnet I, which, when pulled by a steamer (a type of boat), was able to carry a man (Lt. Thomas Selfridge) 168 feet above the water for seven minutes before falling into the water.

Fun Stuff

The Alexander Graham Bell National Historic Site in Baddeck is a great place to visit if you're interested in science, cool inventions, or Alexander Graham Bell himself. Explore the museum, take a tour, or do a workshop. *www.pc.gc.ca/en/lhn-nhs/ ns/grahambell*

39

In the early 1900s, the most luxurious hotel east of Montreal was in a coal-mining town in Cape Breton.

Not far from Sydney, Cape Breton, there's a ghost town called Broughton. All that's left now are a few old building foundations, but in the early 1900s it was a busy place. The town was founded by the Cape Breton Coal, Iron & Railway Company, which was owned by two men from England— Thomas Lancaster and Horace Mayhew.

After realizing how much coal was in the area, the pair started making plans to build what they hoped would become a wildly successful mining town. They hired an architect from PEI named William Harris, and in 1905 they started construction on a town that could hold ten thousand people.

This photo of the luxurious Broughton Arms Hotel was taken around 1914, about ten years after the town was built. (Beaton Institute)

49

Among other things, a map of the town shows a railway station, a main office, assistant manager's house, and two big hotels: the Crown Hotel and the Broughton Arms Hotel.

Unfortunately, the town never took off as planned because there were problems shipping the coal. The town wasn't inhabited for very long—only in its very beginnings, and again when First World War soldiers stayed there for a few months in 1916.

Pictures of the Broughton Arms Hotel show a massive structure with a porch that wraps around almost half of the building. There are even a couple of turrets. Some claim that the hotel also featured the first revolving door in North America, although that seems pretty unlikely, since New York's first revolving doors showed up in 1899, when Broughton didn't even exist yet. But even if it wasn't the very first, a revolving door on a hotel in a town that no one ever really lived in is still pretty interesting.

Fun Stuff

You can still explore Broughton today. Just north of Loon Lake, you will find the ruins of the buildings that once stood there. Visit with a parent or another adult, and try to imagine what it looked like in the early 1900s. If you don't live nearby, you can find photos by visiting the Beaton Institute's website (*www.beatoninstitute.com*) and searching for "Broughton."

40

In 1906, Mabel P. French fought for her right to practice law.

To really understand what a big deal this is, you need to know this first: at the time, when legal documents referred to "persons," the term didn't include women. Of course this was ridiculous, but that didn't change until 1929, when five Canadian women took the Attorney General of Canada to court for the right to serve on the Senate—which meant that the word "person" would need to start including women, *all of the time*. That's why this court case is known now as The Persons Case.

There is, of course, a lot more to The Persons Case then that, but that's all you need to know to understand what Mabel French was dealing with.

Mabel, who was born in Saint John, New Brunswick, graduated from King's College Law School in 1902 (King's College Law School later evolved into the University of New Brunswick's Faculty of Law). But for lawyers, that's just one of the first steps towards actually getting to practice law. If you want to become a lawyer, you also have to spend time as an articled clerk (a kind of on-the-job training for lawyers where a practicing lawyer supervises you), and then apply for admission to the bar (this just means getting approval to legally practice law in a specific province).

This last part is where Mabel ran into problems. When she finished her articling in 1905, she applied for admission to the New Brunswick Bar. But because of six judges, she was turned down because the term "persons" in the relevant legal documentation did not include women, and therefore women couldn't practice law.

Mabel French fought to become the first female lawyer in both New Brunswick and British Columbia. (Public Domain)

But Mabel had no intentions of giving up. She decided to stop paying some of her bills so that when the people she owed sued her, she could argue that you can't pay your bills unless you're a person. Fair enough.

Learn More

A lot of things have changed for girls since The Persons Case in 1929. But it's taken a long time, and even now there are things that need fixing. Ask your grandmother or an older female relative what it was like being a girl when she was growing up. What was different? What was the same?

Although she lost the case and (we assume) paid her bills, her point was made. In 1906, legislature was changed so that women could practice law, and French became New Brunswick's first female lawyer.

Unfortunately, French had to start her fight all over again when she moved to British Columbia in 1910. Two years later, after going through the courts again, she won the right for women to practice law in BC, and became the first female lawyer in that province, too.

41

In 1907, Nova Scotia set the first speed limit in Canada.

About thirty years after the first motor vehicle was invented, Nova Scotia became the first Canadian province to set a speed limit. It was passed on April 25, 1907, as a part of the province's first Motor Vehicle Act (or "An Act in Relation to the Registration and Identification of Motor Vehicles and the use of the Public Highways by such Vehicles"). For the record, a "public highway" at the time was very different from what we call a highway today—the act includes "any highway, public street, alley, park, or public space."

The act was very specific. The speed limit for urban areas with a lot of people and buildings was "one mile in eight minutes," the limit for the less populated urban areas was "one mile in five minutes," and the limit for rural areas was "one mile in four minutes." On a bridge? Better not go faster than one mile in fifteen minutes.

And if you were caught speeding you'd have to pay for it, just like you would now. A first offense was $50 or under, a second offense was $100 or less, and a third offense could either cost you $200 or land you in prison for up to sixty days.

Fun Stuff

Want to see some of the oldest motor vehicles in Atlantic Canada? Visit the Nova Scotia Museum of Industry in Stellarton, and see Nova Scotia's first gas-powered car and the first Volvo built in Canada. *www.museumofindustry.novascotia.ca*

42

Anne of Green Gables was rejected 5 times before being published in June 1908.

If you haven't read it, seen the TV show, or watched the musical, you've probably at least heard of L. M. Montgomery's *Anne of Green Gables*. But in case you haven't, it's a novel about an orphaned girl named Anne who moves to Avonlea, Prince Edward Island, to live with Marilla and Matthew Cuthbert, who adopt her.

After the book was published, it became incredibly popular. Magazines and newspapers across Canada and the US gave *Anne of Green Gables* wonderful reviews, saying things like, "Beyond doubt, *Anne of Green Gables* is well worth reading. If you wish to see how really clever an Island girl can be, just get this book" (*Summerside Journal*, July 29, 1908). Within the first six years, the book was reprinted thirty-eight times, selling more than nineteen thousand copies. Now, there are more than 50 million copies in print.

But it took a lot of work to get that far. In addition to writing the book in the first place, Montgomery had to have it typed (she originally wrote it by hand). Then she submitted it to five publishers, including:

- Bobbs-Merrill in Indianapolis
- Macmillan in New York
- Lothrop, Lee, and Shepard in Boston
- Henry Holt in New York
- L. C. Page Company in Boston

They all rejected it. Montgomery put the book away for a little while, but eventually sent it out again to the L.C. Page Company. This time they accepted and published it, and the rest is history.

Fun Stuff

Whether you've read the book and still want more Anne, or you like your book characters better when they're singing and dancing, check out *Anne of Green Gables—The Musical* at Charlottetown's Confederation Centre of the Arts. *www.confederationcentre.com*

43

Michael Thomas won the Charlottetown Patriot Race 3 years in a row, beginning in 1909.

Michael Thomas was always an athletic kid. While he was growing up in Lennox Island First Nation, he participated in a lot of sports, including rugby and speed skating. But he didn't start running competitively until he was almost twenty-five years old, when he ran—and won—a ten-mile event in 1909 called the Charlottetown Patriot Race. Thousands of people were there to see it happen. After that, he joined the Abegweit Track and Field Team.

Over the next few years, Michael won race after race around Atlantic Canada. He won two more Charlottetown Patriot Races, in 1910 and 1911. He also won three consecutive races in Halifax—the 1910, 1911, and 1912 *Halifax Herald-Mail* 10 Mile Road Races. The Halifax race was even more popular than the Charlottetown one—in those years there were usually between 25,000 and 35,000 spectators. By now, Michael had earned a nickname: The Island Longboat. The name was a reference to Thomas Charles Longboat, a record-breaking runner from Six Nations.

In 1911, Michael did something else to cement his place in the history books—he became the first Islander to run the Boston Marathon. Unfortunately that race didn't go overly well for him. His assistant, who was carrying Michael's water, crashed his bike early on. This affected Michael's time, because he had to go without fluids for much of the marathon.

Michael retired in 1912, but he's still celebrated today, with a place in the PEI Sports Hall of Fame and a statue in Stratford, Prince Edward Island.

Fun Stuff

Love to run? If you're anywhere near Stratford, test your racing abilities at the Michael Thomas Race Day, an annual event that includes a ten-mile run, a five-kilometre fun run, and a one-mile run for kids. *www.peisportshalloffame.ca/inductees/michael-thomas*

44

When the *Titanic* sank in April 1912, they didn't fill the lifeboats.

*C*hances are good you already know a lot about the RMS *Titanic*, the famous "unsinkable ship" that sank after hitting an iceberg about 400 miles off the coast of Newfoundland. A big part of that tragic story (and you might know this already) is the fact that even though there were around 2,200 people on board, they didn't have enough lifeboats on the ship for everyone. In fact, they only had 2 wooden cutters that could carry 40 people each, 14 wooden lifeboats that could carry 65 people each, and 4 collapsible lifeboats that could carry 47 people each. That's enough to carry only 1,178 people to safety in the event of an emergency.

But what you might not know is that they didn't even bother to fill the lifeboats they did have. The first lifeboat was dropped about an hour after the ship hit the iceberg. This was one of the wooden lifeboats that could hold 65 people. It left with 28 people—less than half of its capacity. Another 65-person boat left with only 12 people. The other lifeboats were also sent off with available space—there were 472 spaces that could have been used, but weren't.

Even sadder is the fact that many people weren't allowed out of their area until after the lifeboats had been launched. The *Titanic* had three "classes"—first, second, and third. The first-class passengers had the nicest area, and the third-class passengers stayed in a much plainer area. When the *Titanic* hit the iceberg, these third-class passengers were treated very badly—even though the passengers had been ordered to abandon ship, they were kept below by some of the ship's stewards. They were eventually allowed on deck, but not many of them made it up in time to get into the lifeboats.

Learn More

Both the Maritime Museum of the Atlantic in Halifax and the Rooms in St. John's have fantastic *Titanic* exhibits. Visit a museum to learn more about this historic disaster.

45

The only all-Black army unit in Canadian history was founded in Pictou on July 5, 1916.

When the First World War began, lots of men volunteered to go overseas and fight. It would still be a long time before women were allowed to sign up, but some men were banned from enlisting as well. Even though Black men had already fought in the American Revolution *and* the War of 1812, it took a while for military officials to welcome their help in the First World War—until the numbers of white men who were enlisting took a big drop in 1916, and they had no choice. There was a lot of prejudice at the time. There still is, unfortunately, but people were a lot louder about it back then.

On July 5, 1916, the governor general received permission to form a segregated military unit. That meant the unit only included Black people and

This photo of soldiers from the No. 2 Construction Battalion was used on a limited edition stamp released by Canada Post in 2016. (Black Cultural Centre for Nova Scotia)

kept them separate from the white soldiers. The battalion was based at the Market Wharf in Pictou, Nova Scotia, before moving to Truro, and was led by Lieutenant-Colonel Daniel H. Sutherland. Reverend William A. White was the honourary captain, and the only Black officer in the battalion. They looked all over the country for battalion members, but five hundred of the recruits came from Nova Scotia. They called the group the No. 2 Construction Battalion.

The battalion boarded the SS *Southland* on March 28, 1917, and sailed from Halifax Harbour to England, and then to France, where it played a very important and dangerous role. During its deployment, the battalion worked with the Canadian Forestry Corps doing logging work, maintaining front-line trenches, and building transportation infrastructure. The battalion, which became known as The Black Battalion, also cared for the wounded and defused land mines.

Learn More

If you're interested in learning more about the role these brave men played in the First World War, you should visit the Army Museum at the Halifax Citadel.
www.armymuseumhalifax.ca

46

The first North American woman to captain a ship was born in Alma in 1916.

Molly Kool's world was very different from what we know today. She was born during the First World War and, growing up, she spent most of her time with her father on his seventy-foot scow (a flat-bottomed boat that was used to haul cargo). The scow was named the *Jean K*, after Molly's older sister.

Molly spent the later part of her childhood and early part of her adult life living through the Great Depression—a time when a lot of people lost their

This photo of Captain Molly Kool (right) was taken in Alma, where she grew up. (Provincial Archives of New Brunswick, P471-1)

jobs. Many people had so little money that they would have to trade food for doctor's services, and a lot of people didn't even have a place to live.

There were still a couple of years of the Great Depression left when Molly applied to the Merchant Marine School in Saint John—at a time when no woman in North America had ever captained a ship. She didn't get into the school the first time, but she tried again and they let her enroll. She earned a mate's certificate first, and in 1939 she got the paperwork she needed to captain a ship.

She was the first woman in North America to become a ship's captain, and it shocked a lot of people at the time. After all, women do all the same kinds of jobs as men now, but it took a long time and a lot of work to get to this point. According to an article in the *New York Times*, Molly Kool was even featured on the *Ripley's Believe it or Not* radio show.

> ## Fun Stuff
> Want to see where Molly Kool grew up? You can—just stop by the entrance to Fundy National Park. Her house was restored and moved there, and now the park holds kitchen parties there—and everyone's invited! For more information, visit *pc.gc.ca* and search "Molly Kool."

47

A stove saved a toddler's life during the Halifax Explosion in 1917.

The Halifax Explosion happened on December 6, 1917, when the SS *Mont Blanc*, a cargo freighter carrying explosives, was hit by the SS *Imo*, in Halifax Harbour. The *Mont Blanc* caught fire, which of course caught the attention of everyone nearby. Anne Liggins and her four-year-old son Edwin Liggins were said to be watching out the front window of their house on Barrington Street when, about twenty minutes later, the *Mont Blanc* exploded. Sadly, Anne and Edwin died, but two members of their family survived. Private Edward Liggins, Edwin's dad, wasn't home because he was

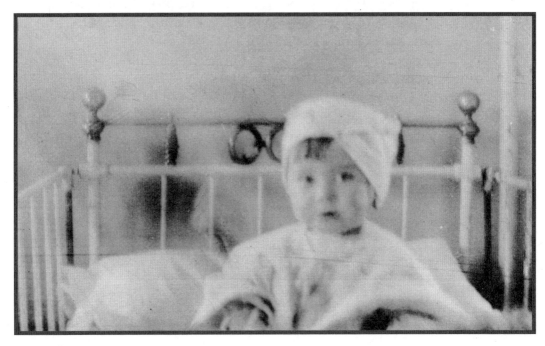

This photo of Annie Liggins was taken shortly after the Halifax Explosion as she recovered in hospital. (Maritime Museum of the Atlantic, MP207.1.184)

at war. But Edwin's little sister, twenty-three-month-old Annie, was home, and when the *Mont Blanc* exploded, the blast pushed her under the stove. At the time, kitchen stoves were a lot different than they are today. They were made from cast-iron, and they worked a lot like a wood stove, but were bigger, and had burners. Since they ran on wood, there were also ashes to deal with—and people did that by sweeping ashes into an ashpan, which was often stored somewhere near the bottom of the stove.

This was very lucky for Annie, because the stove ended up protecting her. Not only did she avoid being seriously burned, the ashpan was just above her, and it still had warm ashes in it. The warmth from these ashes kept her warm during the blizzard that followed the explosion.

More than a day later, she was discovered by a soldier, Benjamin Henneberry, who was looking for his own family. He brought Annie to the Pine Hill Convalescent Hospital where she was eventually found by her grandmother and aunt.

Annie lived a long life. She eventually married, became Annie Welsh, and had children of her own. She spent most of her life living in the Hydrostone District, a community built in Halifax's North End following the explosion, and passed away at the Berkeley Gladstone Seniors Home at the age of ninety-five.

> ### Learn More
> If you want more information about the Halifax Explosion, the Maritime Museum of the Atlantic is the place to go to see artifacts, collect information, and maybe even catch a bit of video footage. *www.maritimemuseum. novascotia.ca/what-see-do/ halifax-explosion*

48

In 1923, Saint John hosted the International Amateur Speed Skating Championships.

Next time you visit Rockwood Park in Saint John, try to imagine the week-long winter carnival that was held there in 1923, from February 10 to 17. The carnival was packed with activities, including tobogganing, bowling and boxing tournaments, hockey and basketball games, a dog show, and a parade.

The biggest event was probably the International Amateur Speed Skating Championships, held on February 14 on Lily Lake. Around twenty thousand people showed up to watch, including Saint John's Winnifred Blair, who had just become the country's first "Miss Canada" four days earlier.

Three years later, the World's Amateur Speed Skating Championships were held in the same place. This time, twenty-five thousand people showed up to watch. This was probably because an Olympic speed skater named Charles Gorman (also from Saint John) was competing. Since he had competed in the Olympics in 1924, this was a pretty big deal. Better yet, the people who showed up to the World's Amateur Speed Skating Championships got to see Gorman win.

Fun Stuff

With lots of trails to explore, plenty of places to mountain bike, beaches, and a great campground, Rockwood Park is still full of fun things to do. It's also in the Stonehammer Geopark site. Find out more at *www.rockwoodpark.ca*.

49

In 1929, Newfoundland was hit by a tsunami.

On November 18, 1929, an earthquake struck Grand Banks, a part of the continental shelf to the southeast of Newfoundland (a continental shelf is the shallow part of ocean floor that's closest to land—the ocean gets much, much deeper the farther out you go). It was a big one, measuring 7.2 on the Richter scale, which means it's the kind of sudden major earthquake that only happens once every fifty years. It was so big that when it happened, places as far away as New York and Portugal recorded tremors.

The earthquake happened under water, but it was disastrous to Newfoundland because it caused an underwater landslide. And that landslide caused a tsunami, which is a series of waves that are so huge they look more like a fast-rising tide than actual waves. They move quickly, too—when the tsunami first formed, it moved towards Newfoundland's Burin Peninsula at one hundred and forty kilometres per hour. When it reached shallower water it slowed down, but it was still

Learn More

Want to hear from the people who lived through the tsunami? Go to *cbc.ca* and check out the video called *Archival moment: Tsunami hits Burin Peninsula* for their stories.

This house was left partially submerged after the tsunami and earthquake on November 18, 1929. (Matilda Kelly Collection, MF-334, Memorial University Archives)

going forty kilometres per hour—about the same speed as the cars that drive through your neighbourhood.

When the tsunami hit the Burin Peninsula, it was so strong that it actually lifted houses off their foundations, caused a million dollars worth of damage, and killed twenty-eight people. Thankfully, many people were able to get out of their houses in time.

50

Until 1930, there was a subspecies of wolf unique to Newfoundland.

There are no wolves in Newfoundland these days, but in the 1800s there were between four hundred and eight hundred grey wolves on the island. According to research, these wolves probably arrived during (and survived through) the Ice Age. This type of wolf was known as the Newfoundland Wolf or, in Latin, *Canis lupus beothucus*, and was a little different from other species of wolves in a few small ways: the carnassials (the teeth they use to slice their prey) were shaped and spaced differently, and the bones in their snouts were a different length.

Until European settlers arrived in Newfoundland, the wolves did well, roaming the island and feasting on a huge caribou population (about 120,000 strong). But by 1925, there were only about 6,000 caribou left—which wasn't enough to support the wolves in the area. There was also a wolf bounty announced in September of 1839—the government offered five pounds sterling for each wolf pelt—but the disappearing wolves were mainly caused by the lack of caribou.

By 1930, the Newfoundland Wolf was completely extinct.

Fun Stuff

Wondering what the Newfoundland Wolf looked like? The Rooms in St. John's has the only known full Newfoundland Wolf pelt on display—go check it out, along with other interesting animal exhibits that feature everything from narwhal tusks to giant squids.
www.therooms.ca

51

Mary Pratt started painting in 1939— when she was 4 years old.

Over the decades, famous artist Mary Pratt has painted a lot of different things. She's painted mangoes, peaches, and pomegranates. She's painted eggs in paper towel and trout in a Ziploc bag. But as ordinary as her subjects seem, there's always a little more to her work than meets the eye— her images have a special way of reminding the viewer of little everyday things and experiences. It's her unique way of seeing and depicting ordinary objects that makes her work so interesting.

Mary started painting and drawing when she was just four years old and living in Fredericton. Even when she was very young, her parents supported her artistic efforts and a few years later, when she was ten and having a tough time, they used her love of art to help her feel better.

"I was no prodigy," Mary once said in an interview. "When I got to be about nine, my parents realized that I was unhappy. I was fat. I didn't know what to do with my hair. I couldn't do math. I liked history and literature. I was truly miserable and they were, 'Well, we'll get her a set of decent paints.' They bought me jars of poster paints, and they were wonderful."

Fun Stuff

Mary Pratt is known for her interesting still life paintings. Create one of your own, but first, have fun arranging the objects you want to paint or draw. Can you find a way to make ordinary objects look special and interesting? For inspiration, view Mary Pratt's work at the Confederation Centre Art Gallery in PEI and The Art Gallery of Nova Scotia.

Despite the fact that she says she "was no prodigy," she must have some natural talent, because she won her first award when she was just ten years old, for a painting called *Sugar Mapling*. About eight years later, she enrolled in the Fine Arts program at Mount Allison University, and about eight years after *that*, she moved to St. John's, Newfoundland, where she still lives today. Since that first award, she's won many others—including Companion of the Order of Canada, the Canada Council of the Arts' Molson Prize, and honourary degrees from a few different universities.

52

Until the 1940s, fox farming was one of Prince Edward Island's biggest moneymakers.

These days hardly anyone wears fur, but for a long time, animal fur was fashionable. And on Prince Edward Island, a lot of people made a lot of money off the trend.

Because silver foxes were rare and hard to get, their fur was worth a lot. In the late 1800s, people started trying to breed them for their pelts. It was around that same time that Charles Dalton and Robert Oulton started breeding silver foxes on Oultons Island. They fenced them in with wire mesh that the foxes had a hard time biting through, and buried the mesh deep enough that they couldn't dig their way out, either.

In 1900, Dalton and Oulton sold one pelt for $1,807, which was an incredible amount of money at the time. Other people discovered they could make money off the rare, beautiful foxes, and over the next ten years the industry grew so large that Prince Edward Island was considered the leader of the silver fox–farming industry. The Island hosted fox shows, and even had an "experimental fox ranch" in Summerside, where different methods of feeding and keeping foxes were tested.

At one point, breeding fox pairs were being sold for as much as $35,000. To help you understand exactly how much money that was: teachers earned between $300 and $1,400 a year at the time.

In the 1940s, fashion trends began to change. Farmers stopped breeding and raising foxes because there was no demand for their fur anymore.

Learn More

Things have changed a lot since the late nineteenth century. Most of us don't use animals as fashion accessories anymore. Instead, we do what we can to protect wildlife—especially species that are rare, endangered, or threatened. But if you want to find out more about the way it was, you can visit the International Fox Museum and Fox Hall of Fame, which are part of the Wyatt Heritage Centre in Summerside, from June to September.

53

In the mid-1900s, nutritionists experimented on Indigenous children in the Shubenacadie Residential School.

Between 1880 and 1996, eighty residential schools were established (at different times) all across Canada. The schools were paid for by the government and run by Christian institutions and missionaries. The people who ran these schools stated that they wanted to help Indigenous children adapt to European-Canadian culture, but instead there was a lot of damage caused to Indigenous communities and individuals.

Indigenous children were taken from their families and forced to live at these schools for ten months a year. They spent half-days in the classroom and half-days working, and their circumstances were miserable—they weren't given good clothing or food, and their teachers didn't support their cultural or spiritual needs. Typically, kids weren't even allowed to speak their own language or send letters home. Often, the children developed serious illnesses, and they were frequently abused by the adults in charge. A lot of children died over the years.

> ### Learn More
> Life in the residential schools was unspeakably hard for most, if not all, of the children who attended them. You can learn more about their experiences by reading books written by former students, including *Fatty Legs* and *A Stranger at Home* by Christy Jordan-Fenton and Margaret Pokiak-Fenton.

Recently, a researcher in Guelph, Ontario, named Ian Mosby discovered that these children, who were already going through so much, were also being used in a nutritional study—and Nova Scotia's Shubenacadie Residential School was one of the places that participated. The study was called "A Long Term Study on Ascorbic Acid Supplementation," and took advantage of the fact that so many of the students weren't getting enough nutritious food. Basically, they let half of the kids go on as usual, and they gave the other half of the kids vitamin C, to see what effects the vitamins would have on them. To make matters worse, they didn't do anything to improve the diets of the children, and they didn't ask the kids or their parents for permission to include them in the study.

54

In March 1945, a woman from Wolfville escaped the Nazis.

Mona Louise Parsons was born in Middleton, Nova Scotia, in 1901. When she was two, she moved to Wolfville with her family (her dad, Colonel Norval Parsons, her mom, Mary Parsons, and her two big brothers). That's where she spent the next seventeen years, until she graduated from the Acadia Ladies' Seminary—where she discovered a love for the arts. She studied to become an actor, and then went to New York to chase her dream. A job as a chorus girl was the closest she got.

Mona Parsons was the honouree for Nova Scotia's 2018 Heritage Day (February 19). (Photo courtesy of Andria Hill)

Eventually, Mona decided to become a nurse instead. She established a successful nursing career in New York, and stayed there until she met her husband, Willem Leonhardt, and they moved to the Netherlands. (Fun fact: their house in the Netherlands was called Ingleside. If you don't know why this is cool, ask someone in your life who is a fan of L. M. Montgomery's books.)

You're probably wondering what all this has to do with Nazis. Well, on September 1, 1939, the Second World War started. Less than a year later, the Nazis occupied Holland (which means, basically, that they took it over). Mona and her husband wanted to do something, so they joined a group that was helping soldiers escape Holland and go back home, wherever home happened to be for them.

Unfortunately, the Nazis discovered what was happening, and on September 29, 1941, Mona was arrested. After spending a brief time in Weteringschane and Amstelveense Prisons, she was moved to Anrath Prison, where she stayed until 1944. That's when she was sent to a work camp for female prisoners of war called Wiedenbrück. A year later, she was sent to Vechta prison camp, where she became friends with a Dutch baroness named Wendelien van Boetzelaer.

On March 24, 1945, the prison was bombed and Mona and Wendelien escaped during the chaos. They made up fake identities, and Mona pretended to be Wendelien's aunt (she was an actress, remember?). The women travelled together for two weeks until they reached the Dutch/German border, where they were separated.

Learn More

There's a lot more to Mona's story than what you've read here. If you want to know more about this fascinating war hero, ask your local librarian to help you find more information. You can also visit her statue, which was erected at the Wolfville post office on May 5, 2017.

Here, Mona stayed with a farming family. The Polish army passed by and told Mona and the family she was staying with to go to Holland, which by then was no longer occupied by Nazis. Together, they crossed the border, and Mona was taken to see the North Nova Scotia Highlanders, an infantry regiment of the Canadian army that happened to be stationed in Holland. She was safe.

55

Built in 1950, Big Tancook Elementary School is one of the last 1-room schoolhouses in Canada.

There are actually two Tancook Islands in Mahone Bay, Nova Scotia—one Big and one Little. Despite its name, Big Tancook is actually pretty little too, at just 4 kilometres long by 1.6 kilometres wide. There are around 110 people living there all year round, and in the summer, the population jumps to about 200.

The islands got their names from the Mi'kmaq, who call it Uktankook, which means "facing the open sea," and were occupied by German and French settlers in 1829. For a long time, one of their primary industries was sauerkraut.

Of course, the children of the (approximately) 110 people who live there all year long need a place to go to school. Until they start grade six, that place is Big Tancook Elementary School, a tiny one-room schoolhouse that averages about ten students a year total, from grades primary to five (after that, kids take the ferry over to Chester for school).

In 2016, when the school dropped to just two students, the South Shore Regional School Board had to vote on whether to keep it open or not. Luckily for those two students, and any younger kids getting ready to start school, they voted to keep it open.

Fun Stuff

Big Tancook Island is a great place for a summer day trip. Take the ferry over from Chester and spend the day walking around, exploring the local beaches, geocaching, and visiting boutiques. You can even rent a bike for the day! Check out *www.tancookislandtourism.ca* for more information.

56

Until the 1950s, the *veillée* (a storytelling event) was common in Newfoundland's French communities.

From the nineteenth century (the 1800s), until TV came along in the 1950s, French Newfoundlanders commonly passed the time by telling each other stories. Many of these stories were folk tales or fairy tales, passed down from generation to generation.

These stories were often told at a kind of kitchen get-together called a *veillée*. Some of these events were held in public, and usually featured talented, well-known storytellers. These stories would sometimes take three hours to tell, and the storyteller would use a lot of the same kinds of techniques actors do—they'd use different voices for different characters, they'd gesture with their hands, and they'd make faces. You might not have been allowed to go to this type of event, though—this kind of gathering was more for adults.

But the private *veillée* was for all ages, and although they don't happen as frequently as they used to, these events still happen today. Because they are mainly family gatherings, they are a lot more casual, and the storytellers are simply parents or grandparents, uncles or aunts, with a story to share. People can interrupt and ask questions, and kids are always welcome.

Fun Stuff

Why not have a storytelling night in your own kitchen? Pick an evening, turn off the TV, and gather up some friends and family. Spend an evening trading your favourite stories—and make sure to have plenty of snacks!

57

In 1955, a "Little Drummer Boy" made a big noise in Charlottetown.

It's always interesting to dig back through old newspapers. They're a great way to learn about events that happened in the past, and they're full of interesting old advertisements. But it's also fun to look through the headlines and see what kinds of things were reported as news. According to a book called *Chinese Islanders: Making a Home in the New World*, a little boy named John William Ling was the talk of Charlottetown, Prince Edward Island, in 1955.

At the time, John was just two years and eight months old, and he attracted the attention of reporters with a daily march through the streets, beating on a toy drum with a couple of sticks. His parents were probably busy working—his dad, William Ling, ran the John Ling Laundry on Grafton Street, and his mom, Leola Tolman, worked there too. The family lived above the shop, so the children would play nearby.

Learn More

John William Ling's grandfather, John Ling, was one of the earliest Chinese immigrants to live in Charlottetown. He arrived on PEI in 1894, which was a very difficult time for Chinese people living in Canada. Most people who came to PEI from China were men, and they had to leave their families behind. Plus, they had to pay a very expensive "Head Tax" of fifty dollars. This tax was only charged to people emigrating from China, and was hard to afford. Fifty dollars was worth a lot more than it is now, and that tax was eventually raised to five hundred dollars. The Canadian Museum of Immigration at Pier 21 in Halifax is a great place to learn the stories of people who have moved to Canada throughout history. If you're in the area, be sure to stop—it's open all year long.
www.pier21.ca

According to the newspapers, John started out marching up and down Queen Street, then stopping at the corner to march in a circle for a while before going home for lunch. Later, the family and the shop moved to 167 ½ Queen Street, and he started marching around the block.

"Setting out from Queen, he would march down Grafton Street, then onto Pownal and Kent before returning to Queen Street," the newspaper says.

The little boy had lots of fans, but he also had a nemesis, an antique dealer who didn't like the sound of the drums at eight o'clock in the morning. The man actually took the little boy to court, claiming that he was disturbing the peace. But the little boy got the last laugh when the judge "sentenced" him to start playing his drums even earlier every morning—at seven thirty!

58

In 1955, a 17-year-old from PEI travelled to Antarctica with Sir Edmund Hillary.

Sir Edmund Hillary was a mountain climber and explorer who was born in New Zealand in 1919. In his lifetime, he did some pretty incredible things. In 1953 he became one of the first two people to reach the top of Mount Everest (he was travelling with a guide named Tenzing Norgay, and they reached the summit together). He was also one of the first people to reach the top of Mount Herschel, in 1967. And in 1985, he flew to the North Pole with Neil Armstrong, who was the first person to walk on the moon.

Why am I telling you all this? So that you'll understand exactly how exciting it must have been for seventeen-year-old Jim Reggie MacDonald when he found out he would get to travel to Antarctica with Hillary. This was in 1955, so Hillary hadn't climbed Mount Herschel or reached the North Pole yet, but he had recently climbed Everest, and MacDonald, who was from Souris, PEI, met him while working on a sealing ship called the MV *Theron*.

According to a January 2016 CBC News article, the company that owned the ship was hired to take supplies to the Antarctic, and so MacDonald went with it. The ship picked up Hillary in Uruguay. After that, MacDonald had a couple of opportunities to spend time with the man who beat Everest—he not only got to join Hillary on a small mountain climbing expedition in South Georgia and the Sandwich Islands, he also went seal hunting with him.

Fun Stuff

Want to climb Mount Everest someday? Start testing your climbing abilities closer to home. All four Atlantic provinces have climbing gyms with special harnesses that will let you climb while making the adventure as safe as possible. Ask your parents which one is closest to you.

59

In 1957, 3 men left Dartmouth to sail a raft across the Atlantic Ocean.

In 1947, a zoologist named Thor Heyerdahl and a few friends crossed the Pacific Ocean—from Peru to French Polynesia—on a forty-foot balsa wood raft he named *Kon-Tiki*. The voyage received a lot of attention, especially after Heyerdahl wrote a book about it, called *The Kon-Tiki Expedition: By Raft Across the South Seas*.

About five years later, a young man named Henri Beaudout, who had moved to Montreal with his wife after fighting in the French resistance (which is what we call the efforts French people made to try and keep the German army out of France in the Second World War) heard about what Heyerdahl had done, and decided to try crossing the Atlantic Ocean. After doing some research on ocean currents and raft materials, he got in touch with the Maritime Telephone and Telegraph company to see if they could help supply telephone poles that he could use for his raft. They helped him out and the raft, which he called *L'Egare II*, French for "World War II," was eventually built out of nine cedar poles tied together. There was a little plywood cabin added to the top, for shelter.

In May of 1956, Beaudout and three friends— Gaston Vanackere, Jose Martinez, and Marc Modena—left Dartmouth, Nova Scotia, and headed out to sea. They brought two kittens along on the journey, too—according to a CBC News article, the men hoped they'd be able to predict storms by watching the cats' behaviour.

Fun Stuff

Can you build your own mini-raft? Start by gathering some different materials— try popsicle sticks, rolled-up paper sticks, or just sticks you find on the ground—and tie them together using string to make a raft. Then get a friend to build a raft from a different material. Try them out on a pond, stream, or even a big puddle, and see which materials float better. Just remember—if you think your raft might float away, use biodegradable materials so that it doesn't turn into litter!

The crew arrived in Falmouth, UK, eighty-eight days later. Everyone made it, except for Martinez, who got sick during the trip and had to get off the raft in Newfoundland. It was pretty exciting when they arrived—the *Globe & Mail* says they were invited out to dinner with a lot of important people, including the Queen of England. They met the Duke of Bedford while they were there, and he adopted the kittens when it was time for Beaudout and his friends to go home.

This is King's Wharf in Dartmouth, Nova Scotia, where L'Egare II *started its voyage.*

60

One of the miners who survived the 1958 Springhill mining disaster wrote a song about the experience.

On October 23, 1958, while miners were hard at work in the Number 2 pit in Springhill, Nova Scotia (which, at 4,262 metres, was actually the deepest pit in North America at the time), a "bump," which is an underground earthquake, caused the mine to collapse, trapping 174 miners underground. There was a major rescue effort over the next few days, and ultimately, 100 miners were saved. The last 7 survivors were rescued on the morning of November 1.

One of the seven survivors was Maurice Ruddick, a forty-six-year-old African Canadian who was known as "The Singing Miner" because he sang and composed songs. He sang a lot while working in the mine, too—leading the other miners in song when they were descending into the mine and coming back up, and during rest times.

According to an article written by Neil V. Rosenberg and published in the *Canadian Folk Music Bulletin*, Ruddick was actually singing a song he had written, called "The Curse of Old Number 2," the morning of the disaster. Despite a broken leg, he tried to keep everyone from losing hope by leading songs underground while the survivors waited for rescue. After he was rescued, he wrote another song, called "Spring Hill Disaster," which described what it was like for the people waiting to be rescued.

Learn More

Maurice Ruddick's story is part of a series of interesting mini-movies about Canadian history, called Heritage Minutes. You've probably seen some of them on TV, but you can also find them all online. Go to *www.historicacanada.ca* and click on "Heritage Minutes."

People all across North America paid attention to the disaster, and when the last few survivors were rescued, Marvin Griffin, the governor of Georgia, decided to offer the last seven rescued miners free vacations to Jekyll Island, a popular tourist spot off the coast of Georgia. Unfortunately and unfairly, when Griffin found out that Ruddick was Black, he wouldn't let Ruddick and his family stay with the other miners—they had to stay in a trailer away from everyone else. The other miners offered to refuse the vacation because they didn't want Ruddick to be segregated, but Ruddick wouldn't let them—he didn't want them to miss out on their vacations.

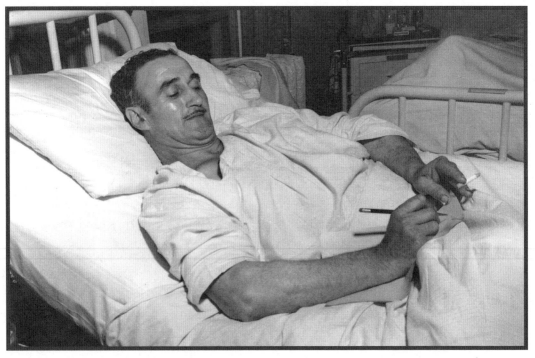

After the mining disaster in 1958, Maurice Ruddick had to recover in the hospital. (Nova Scotia Archives)

61

In June 1963, a very unlucky circus arrived in Yarmouth.

In the early 1960s, the Al G. Kelly and Miller Brothers Circus bought a freighter (a ship designed to transport goods). Instead of using it to move product, they used the *Fleurus* to move circus animals. Specifically, they used it to move lions, leopards, bears, llamas, ponies, horses, zebras, dogs, three elephants, a cheetah, and a Brahma bull (which looks like a large, lumpy cow).

On June 1, 1963, the *Fleurus* was supposed to leave St. Petersburg, Florida, for Canada. Unfortunately, the crew ended up spending the day chasing down an escaped elephant and two ponies. As for the captain, he spent *his* day recovering from the cuts he got when he walked into a glass door.

The *Fleurus* did set sail on June 2, but her luck didn't get any better. Since they put all three elephants on the same side (starboard), the boat leaned heavily to that side, and the steering mechanism ended up breaking. Within a couple of days, it was fixed and they set sail again, but then a piston cracked, the radio went dead, and their refrigeration system broke—which means most

Thanks to the fire department and other helpers, almost all the animals were rescued from the fire on board the Fleurus. *(Courtesy of the Yarmouth County Museum Archives)*

of the food went bad. After a repair-related detour to South Carolina, the freighter finally arrived in Yarmouth, Nova Scotia, where the circus put on two performances.

The newspaper ad, dated Tuesday June 11, makes the show (which was sponsored by the Auspices Fire Department) sound pretty exciting. Not only does it advertise a special performance by a man named Captain Eddy and his "MAN-KILL-ING JUNGLE-BRED LIONS," it also says: "This is positively the first and only large Circus ever to be transported from town to town on its own ocean-going diesel motored ship. Be at dockside to see this great Circus unload."

The performances went off without a hitch. But then the ship's engine room caught on fire. With the help of the (sponsoring) fire department, a crane, a veterinarian, and a lot of helpers, all the animals were saved—except for one zebra—but the ship was destroyed.

Learn More

Want to learn more about Yarmouth's fire department? Then you're in luck. Visit the Firefighters' Museum of Nova Scotia to check out actual firefighting equipment and learn about people who risk their lives to save other people (and sometimes animals). *www.firefightersmuseum. novascotia.ca*

62

Tide Head, which officially became a village in 1966, calls itself the Fiddlehead Capital of the World.

And it might be right. According to people who live in the small New Brunswick town, fiddleheads are as common as dandelions in the springtime—popping up all over the yards and forested areas. But you don't just find fiddleheads on the ground in Tide Head—they've also incorporated the fiddlehead into their town crest, which is a picture of Morrissey Rock and the Restigouche River, surrounded by a frame that says *Village of/ de Tide Head*. The frame is topped with a green maple leaf, and fiddleheads on either side. There are also fiddleheads on the New Brunswick coat of arms.

Of course, fiddleheads are common all over the Atlantic provinces, and people have been foraging for them for hundreds of years. The Maliseet First Nation in New Brunswick have always harvested them for medicine, and much more recently (but still for a pretty long time), people have been cooking and serving them as vegetables.

Another fun fact about fiddleheads: the fiddleheads themselves are actually only the curled-up top part of a fern—not the name of the actual plant. The edible ones come from a plant called the ostrich fern, and the curled-up tops are called fiddleheads for a very simple reason—because they look like a fiddle!

Fun Stuff

Next spring, go out looking for fiddleheads! But be careful—make sure you bring an adult who knows a lot about plants. There are many different types of ferns, and not all fiddleheads can be eaten. Once you've collected enough to cook, make sure you wash them extremely well. And ask an adult to help you cook them—they have to be cooked very well too, or they could make you sick.

63

Until the early 1960s, New Brunswick had a passenger train with a ghostly nickname.

Have you ever heard of the Dungarvon Whooper? If not, you probably don't live anywhere near Miramichi, because he's pretty well known around those parts.

In the late nineteenth century, there was a logging camp near the Dungarvon River. According to local folklore, the camp had a cook who wasn't just responsible for feeding everyone but also for using his loud, bellowing voice to call messages across the river, waking the loggers up in the morning, and singing songs by the campfire at night.

Unfortunately, the cook was killed one night, probably because of the moneybelt he carried around his waist. According to a poem written by Michael Whelan, when the cook was found, his moneybelt was empty. There are a few different versions of the story, but they usually involve the theft of the moneybelt. In most versions, a storm hit just after the cook was killed, and the loggers quickly buried him in a shallow grave in the woods.

According to legend, the cook haunts the woods in the area, but his ghost is pretty harmless—he just does a lot of screaming and yelling. That's why the ghost is called the Dungarvon Whooper—because of all the noise it's said to make. Some people have even chalked the noises up to mountain lions. But the legend lives on, and for a while, there was even a passenger train nicknamed the Dungarvon Whooper after the ghost—because people said the train's whistle sounded like the ghost's wailing. The train ran from Newcastle to Fredericton until the early 1960s.

Fun Stuff

If the ghost story has captured your imagination, why not explore the area with a parent? If you can't find the actual logging site, visit the town of Blackville instead and check out the chainsaw statue of the cook himself (pre-ghost).

64

The Shag Harbour Incident wasn't the only UFO sighting in the area in the 1960s.

Around eleven o'clock at night on October 4, 1967, Shag Harbour residents got quite a surprise when a really large object (about sixty feet across) hovered over Shag Harbour, flashed its lights, and then, with a flash and a bang, crashed into the water. Of course, people thought an aircraft of some kind had crashed into the water, and they started calling the RCMP. RCMP officers arrived on the scene, and some caught a glimpse of the object before it sank to the bottom of the harbour.

Afterwards, RCMP conducted a search—for the object and any survivors—but nothing was found. It's all very mysterious.

But according to the records of Aerial Phenomena Research Organization (APRO), a former UFO research group in Wisconsin, there was another UFO crash just a few months later, close to the same place.

At around eight o'clock at night on May 4, 1968, a fishing boat captain named Woodrow Atwood was near Seal Island when he saw a pinprick of light in the sky to the north of his boat. According to his report, the pinprick burst into a "blood red light" that looked like it was floating towards the boat. It passed over the boat and kept going, but Atwood made sure to tell people how hot it felt as it went by—he said it was so hot that he worried it would burn the boat.

> **Fun Stuff**
> Interested in UFOs? Be sure to make a visit to the Shag Harbour Incident Society Museum to check out stories, photos, and artifacts. If you time it right, you might even be there for the Shag Harbour UFO Incident Festival. *www.cuun.i2ce.com/misc/shagHarbourMuseum*

65

PEI has been shrinking by 28 centimetres a year since 1968.

You've probably learned about global warming in school. And if you have, then you know that the Arctic ice is melting really, *really* fast. If you're interested in numbers, that's 13.3 percent-every-ten-years fast. And of course, when Arctic ice melts, sea levels rise all over the world.

Fun Stuff

Did you know that when an ice cube melts in a glass of water, the water level doesn't change? That's because when water freezes, it expands by about 9 percent. When it melts, it contracts (takes up less space), which means the water levels even out. Want to see it for yourself? Try this experiment. All you'll need is a glass, water, an ice cube, and a ruler.

Step 1: Pour the water in the glass, but make sure to leave a couple of inches at the top.

Step 2: Add the ice cube.

Step 3: Measure from where the water meets the bottom of the glass to the surface of the water.

Step 4: Write down your measurement, and give the ice a chance to melt.

Step 5: Once the ice has melted, measure the water again and compare your findings.

Sea levels are rising for two reasons:

1. Climate change is warming the oceans, and as the water warms to about 4 degrees or higher, it expands—and that means it takes up more space.

2. Climate change is also melting ice that's been on land for millions of years. The melted ice runs off the land and into the oceans, making the water levels rise.

And as these water levels rise, they start affecting the land—like Prince Edward Island for example.

Recently, researchers from the University of Prince Edward Island and Simon Fraser University in British Columbia released the results of a study that examined the effects of erosion (when the edges of a chunk of land wears away because of storms, rising sea levels, and melting ice) on PEI from 1968 until 2010. Their discovery? That the island has lost twenty-eight centimetres a year during that time period. That's a lot of land—and it all adds up.

NOVA SCOTIA

66

There's an Avco World Trophy from the 1970s in the Nova Scotia Sport Hall of Fame.

If you've never heard of the Avco World Trophy, that's because the World Hockey Association (WHA) doesn't exist anymore. But from 1972 to 1979, it was a pretty huge deal.

The National Hockey League (NHL) is probably one of the first things that comes to mind when you think about professional hockey. But in the 1970s, the World Hockey Association was a popular league too—so popular that Gordie Howe came out of retirement to play for one of their teams (the Houston Aeros). Wayne Gretzky also scored his first goal as a professional hockey player while playing for a WHA team called the Indianapolis Racers.

> ### Fun Stuff
>
> Visit the Nova Scotia Sport Hall of Fame in Halifax and see one of the Avco World Trophies for yourself. When you visit, be sure to check out the names on the trophy and see if there are any you recognize.

Unfortunately, the WHA ran into money trouble and shut down in 1979. But even though the association didn't last long, there are still bits and pieces left today. They had three Avco trophies, which looked a lot like the Stanley Cup, except for the globe in the middle. Those trophies are all on

Check out this Avco World Trophy at the Nova Scotia Sport Hall of Fame in downtown Halifax. (Nova Scotia Sport Hall of Fame)

display in different provinces—one in the Manitoba Sports Hall of Fame and Museum, one in the Nova Scotia Sport Hall of Fame, and one in the Hockey Hall of Fame in Toronto.

They also left behind a few teams. The Edmonton Oilers were originally a WHA team. And the New England Whalers, Winnipeg Jets, and Quebec Nordiques all moved to the NHL and eventually became the Carolina Hurricanes, the Arizona Coyotes, and the Colorado Avalanche.

67

Beginning in the 1970s, PEI had some strict rules about drinks in aluminum cans or plastic bottles.

For about thirty years, PEI had a ban on drinks sold in non-reusable containers. There were a bunch of reasons for this, but most of them had to do with the environment. First, it takes more energy to recycle an aluminum can than to refill a glass bottle, and even though you can recycle cans you still can't reuse all the materials. The province also wanted to cut down on litter, and glass is a more natural product than aluminum or plastic, so sticking to glass was a good option. As a bonus, it also meant that the Island's glass-bottling plant got more business. In 1984, pop cans were banned, too.

But in the 2000s, people started to complain. They really, really wanted cans. They wanted them so badly, in fact, that they signed petitions asking for the can ban to be lifted, and political parties actually promised to bring back cans during an election campaign.

So in 2007, the people got their wish and the can ban was lifted. For the first time in decades, they could buy drinks in aluminum cans and plastic bottles on the Island. The government tried to counter some of the environmental impact by introducing blue boxes, so that people could recycle their aluminum cans and plastic bottles.

Fun Stuff

Can you think of a creative way to reuse a bottle or can? Take a look around the house for small items like buttons, beads, googly eyes, pipe cleaners, and anything else you think you might be able to use, and get creative! Add eyes and pipe cleaners to turn your can into a robot, or fill your bottle with beads and make some music. The possibilities are endless!

68

At least 9 cars have driven into the same New Brunswick house since 1971.

Maureen and Terry Noble live in the quiet town of Tracy, New Brunswick. But their yard isn't so peaceful. Since they moved in, in 1971, their house has been hit by so many cars they can't even remember exactly how many collisions there have been. The problem seems to be a speeding issue. They live on a sharp turn on Heritage Drive and instead of driving thirty kilometres per hour around the curve like they're supposed to, a lot of drivers are going eighty kilometres per hour. Going this fast around the turn causes the drivers to lose control of the car, go off the road, and land in the front part of the Nobles' house.

When the problem first started—almost five decades ago—that front area was a Canada Post office. Maureen Noble was the town's postmaster, and the office was attached to her house. According to the *Canadian Press,* a car hit the house in 2007 while she was watching TV in her living room, and she had to move everything from the post office into her house. In 2009 another car hit the same area, and part of the living room where Terry was napping.

> ### Fun Stuff
> Next time you go for a long drive, pay attention to the road signs. Can you guess what they mean? Ask an adult to tell you if your guesses are correct. Or have some fun by making up the funniest interpretations you can think of!

The Nobles are hoping that the Department of Transportation and Infrastructure (the part of the government that takes care of things like roads and bridges) will do something to protect their house. In 2007, they lowered the speed limit and put up a sign to warn drivers, but the Nobles are hoping the government will also put in a guardrail or a flashing light.

69

George Elliott Clarke first started writing poetry in 1975, as a way to stand out in high school.

It was the summer after George graduated from junior high, where he'd earned a reputation for being a great student. He was about to start high school in Halifax, and since there are a lot more students in high school, he knew that if he wanted teachers to keep noticing him he'd need more than just good grades. And he wasn't athletic, so sports weren't an option.

He'd always loved music, so he decided to start writing song lyrics. He took it really seriously and practiced a lot, writing four songs every day for about two or three years. He also did a lot of reading about songwriting, and as he did, he realized how song lyrics are basically a form of poetry. After he made that connection, he started writing different kinds of poetry, too.

George's goal worked—he did stand out to his teachers, and they ended up doing what they could to help him become a better poet. Since then, he's earned all kinds of recognition and awards, including the Governor-General's Award for Poetry (2001), the Dr. Martin Luther King Jr. Achievement Award (2004), and an appointment to the rank of Officer in the Order of Canada (2008). In 2016, many years after he first started writing songs, George Elliott Clarke became the Parliamentary Poet Laureate of Canada.

Learn More

Everyone is good at something. Some people bake delicious cookies, other people have an ear for music. Some people have a lot of artistic talent, and others are amazing soccer players. What's your thing? Jot down some of the activities you really love, and pick the one you love most. Then, try to set aside a couple of times a week to practice—getting good at something you love will make you happier and more confident.

70

On Groundhog Day in 1976, one of Atlantic Canada's worst winter storms hit New Brunswick and Nova Scotia.

February 2, 1976, started out as a regular day in Atlantic Canada—but that all changed when two big storms teamed up over New England and headed to Canada. The storm arrived in the Bay of Fundy with winds of about 188 kilometres per hour, creating 12-metre-high waves—with swells of about 10 metres. According to the Saffir-Simpson Hurricane Wind Scale, these kinds of winds are equivalent to a Category 3 hurricane.

Saint John, New Brunswick, was hit worse than any other area in eastern Canada. The winds were so high they snapped power poles, blew the roofs off houses, and splashed salt water on houses six miles from the ocean. The storm also tore sheets of plywood off a construction project in the city, which caused even more damage when the plywood blew away and hit cars and buildings.

A life was lost that day too—a man was killed when his fishing shack was blown across the Kennebecasis River.

By the time the storm was over, docks were damaged, the lighthouse at Fish Fluke Point was destroyed, a large part of a sea wall caved in, and a barge in Courtenay Bay slammed into the Courtenay Bay Causeway. Overall, the storm caused more than $8 million in damages.

Even the groundhog didn't see that coming.

Learn More

Over the last couple of decades, Atlantic Canada has experienced a lot of interesting weather. Talk to your parents and ask them what they remember about these weather events:

- New Brunswick's 2003 ice storm
- Hurricane Juan
- White Juan
- The 2008 Saint John River flood
- Hurricane Igor

71

Founded in 1978, Canada's oldest children's bookstore is in Halifax.

On Birmingham Street in Halifax, there's a bright yellow building with a green door. In the window, there could be almost anything—from a winter wonderland full of snowman stuffies and fairy puppets to a pink paradise filled with books about bullying. Take a left after walking through the front doors and you'll find a treasure trove of toys. Turn right, and you'll find books for all ages, and on just about any topic a kid would ever want to know about.

This is Woozles Children's Bookstore, the oldest children's bookstore in Canada. It was founded in 1978 by Ann Connor Brimer, and Liz and Brian Crocker, and quickly became a popular place to have a birthday party, attend a workshop, and, of course, pick out a really great book. It also developed a reputation for having the best stickers in the city. The first manager was Trudy Carey, and it's now co-managed by Lisa Doucet (who's been there for ages and knows all the best young adult books) and Suzy

Woozles Children's Bookstore, on Birmingham Street, has been Halifax's best spot for kids' books since it opened in 1978.

MacLean (Liz and Brian's youngest daughter, who sometimes calls Woozles her big sister).

It's a remarkable place, mostly because of the great books and toys, the friendly booksellers, and the big comfy chair in the back. But it's also impressive because, sadly, it's one of the few remaining independent bookstores in Halifax—and there used to be many more.

Fun Stuff

Go to Woozles! From writing contests to events, there's always something happening. Find out more here: *www.woozles.com.*

72

In 1983, Marvel introduced Marrina, a superhero born in Newfoundland.

In the Marvel Universe, there's an alien race called the Plodex, who left their home planet when they used up all of its natural resources (water, vegetation, rich soil, things like that). They started taking over other planets, using all of *their* natural resources too. Whenever those planets ran out of resources, the Plodex would abandon them and go looking for a new place to use up. They did this for hundreds of years before eventually focusing on Earth.

They tried to take over Earth by scattering thousands of eggs all over the world, but most of those were killed by the Ice Age. However, one egg did survive and landed near Newfoundland, where it was found by a fisherman named Tom Smallwood a few millennia later. The fisherman brought it home with him and showed it to his wife. It hatched, and Marrina emerged, a small human-shaped creature with yellowish skin, green hair, gills, and webbed hands and feet. She also turned out to have water-related powers, like super-speedy swimming skills and the ability to survive at extreme ocean depths (most people can't do so without oxygen tanks—that's why diving is sometimes dangerous).

When Marrina was old enough, her adoptive father told the Canadian government about her and Marrina joined Gamma Flight (a training program for Canadian superheroes). She eventually became a part of Alpha Flight—a superhero team that included Wolverine during its early days.

Fun Stuff

Want to meet the real artists, writers, and actors behind your favourite superheroes? Check out one of Atlantic Canada's comic conventions: Atlanti-Con, Avalon Expo, and Sci-fi on the Rock in Newfoundland; Hal-Con, Geequinox, and Dartmouth Comic Arts Festival in Nova Scotia; and Animaritime and East Coast Comic Expo in New Brunswick.

73

Bernard DeGrâce started officiating hockey games in the 1980s—because he needed to pay for university.

On June 4, 2016, NHL officiator Bernard (Bernie) DeGrâce, who was born in Shippagan, was inducted into the New Brunswick Sports Hall of Fame. Over twelve years, from 1989 to 2002, he refereed more than 980 hockey games—and 350 of those were for the NHL.

He started out as a linesman, after one of his friends brought him to an officiating clinic. Since Bernie was in school at the Université de Moncton, he was happy for the chance to earn some money to put towards his tuition. (Tuition is the money you pay to go to university. And university costs *a lot*.) Luckily, Bernie turned out to be really good at officiating. Another officiator named Romeo LeBlanc noticed this, and helped Bernie get work as a linesman in the AHL. Before long, he started working as a linesman with the NHL, too. Then, a few years later, his career took another big step and he became a referee for the NHL.

All this is impressive, but Bernie has two more claims to fame: he's the first New Brunswick referee and the first Acadian referee/linesman to officiate in the NHL.

Fun Stuff

Want to try a new sport? Visit the New Brunswick Sports Hall of Fame's Virtual Sports Simulator and try your hand (or foot) at baseball, basketball, football, hockey, and soccer. Of course, while you're there, you should also check out the Biomechanics and Sports Discovery Centre. *www.nbsportshalloffame.com*

74

In 1989, a group of kids collected the rocks and bricks included in Dartmouth's World Peace Pavilion.

The World Peace Pavilion in Dartmouth, Nova Scotia, displays rocks and bricks from all over the world. While the pavilion itself was designed by adults (an architecture firm called Robert Parker Associates) and dedicated by adults (seven foreign ministers who were attending the Halifax G7 Summit

The World Peace Pavilion is open to visitors in the summer, but you can check it out any time at Alderney Landing. If you're in Halifax, why not take the ferry over to Dartmouth?

in 1995), the original idea came from Metro Youth for Global Unity, a group of kids who lived in Dartmouth and wanted a way to promote world peace and harmony.

In 1989, the group wrote letters to every country in the world and asked them to send a rock or a brick from something important about their country. A whole bunch of countries responded, including Japan, Sri Lanka, China, Finland, Yugoslavia, Croatia, France, Ireland, Kuwait, Iceland, Qatar, Israel, Libya, Malawi, Haiti, and many, many more. Some of the most interesting rocks and bricks include:

- two pieces of basalt rock that were excavated when the world's largest tunnel was being built (in Japan);
- a rock and a brick from the Great Wall of China;
- a brick from a Finnish castle;
- a piece of lava rock found in Iceland;
- two stones from Mount Kilimanjaro (the highest mountain in Africa);
- rubble from a US nuclear silo.

Fun Stuff
Visit Alderney Landing in Dartmouth and see the World Peace Pavilion for yourself. Go on the right day, and you might even catch a market or a festival. *www.alderneylanding.com*

75

There's a time capsule hidden inside the giant axe that was built in Nackawic in 1991.

Every year, the Canadian Forestry Association announces a new Forest Capital of Canada. In 1991, it was Nackawic, New Brunswick. The town celebrated in a big way—by building the world's biggest axe. The axe, which is a little over eighteen metres long and seven metres wide, was designed and manufactured by B.I.D. Canada Ltd. in Woodstock. In the head of the axe, there's a time capsule that will supposedly be opened on the fiftieth

This giant axe is fifteen metres tall! That's almost fifty feet—about as tall as five giraffes, or two school buses. (Can Stock)

anniversary of the axe—which seems a little odd since you'd probably need an axe to get into the time capsule.

There are also many other giant objects and animals scattered around Atlantic Canada, including:

- World's Largest Conch Shell in Caraquet, NB
- Harvey's Big Potato in Maugerville, NB
- Blowhard the Bony Horse in Penobsquis, NB
- World's Largest Blueberry in Oxford, NS
- Mastodon in Stewiacke, NS
- World's Largest Fiddle in Sydney, NS
- Woven Basket in Richmond, PEI
- Giant Squid in Glovers Harbour, NL
- Cressie the Crescent Lake Monster in Roberts Arm, NL

76

The McDonald's McFlurry was invented in Bathurst, New Brunswick, in 1995.

In 1995, a man named Ron McLellan, who owned two McDonald's restaurants in Bathurst, added a new dessert to his menu: the McFlurry. As you probably know, the treat is soft-serve ice cream blended with pieces of candy, like Smarties, Oreos, or Rolos. People loved the sweet new treat, and before long McDonald's decided to add it to its menus all over the country.

In 1998, McDonald's began selling McFlurrys in the US, and now the delicious dessert is available at McDonald's restaurants all over the world—but the ingredients change from place to place. International flavours have included:

- Baci (Italy)
- Banana Toffee (Malaysia)
- Black Liquorice (Finland)
- Blueberry Oreo (Japan)
- Bubblegum Squash (Australia and New Zealand)
- Pineapple Oreo (Colombia)
- Matcha Green Tea (Japan)
- Red Bean (China)
- Toblerone (Switzerland)

Fun Stuff

If you've got a blender and all the right ingredients, you can make your own ice cream treat at home! Go online (with a parent's permission, of course) and search for a soft-serve ice cream recipe. Lots of them will say to use a "soft-serve ice cream maker," but you don't need one—you can use a blender, too. Once you've made the ice cream, mix in extra ingredients of your choice—like chocolate, cookies, or fruit. Have fun—if you can imagine it, you can do it!

77

The world's oldest known intact shark fossil was found near Campbellton in 1997.

In 1997 Randall Miller, a paleontologist (a scientist who studies fossils) from the New Brunswick Museum took a team of scientists on a field expedition just outside of Campbellton, New Brunswick. They were looking for teeth from the *Doliodus problematicus,* a species of shark from the Devonian era (which spanned about 416 million to 358 million years ago). And they definitely found what they were looking for—and a whole lot more.

During the expedition, a student found a complete *Doliodus problematicus* fossil. It's twenty-three centimetres long, and 409 million years old—which is at least 15 million years older than previously discovered shark fossils. According to a *National Geographic* article, the fossil included scales, cartilage, parts of the fish's fins, and teeth that were still attached to the fish's jaws.

> ### Fun Stuff
>
> If you're interested in the Devonian period (also known as the Age of Fishes), you should visit Sugarloaf Provincial Park in Campbellton. The park has lots of hiking trails, a campground, and Sugarloaf Mountain, which is actually an extinct volcano from the Devonian period.

This fossil was a really important find, and over the years it's been studied by scientists from all over the world. It's also giving scientists new information about ancient sharks. For example, from this fossil, they've learned that sharks had fin spines in their pectoral fins (those are the fins on the side of a shark).

78

People first started commercially harvesting Newfoundland icebergs in the 1990s.

Every year, in spring and the early part of summer, Newfoundland gets some giant visitors. If you visit Iceberg Alley, which runs along the coast of Labrador down to northeast coast of Newfoundland, during that time of year, you're almost sure to see an iceberg or two or more travelling past.

The icebergs are beautiful, but people enjoy them for more than the view.

Giant icebergs like this one are found in Newfoundland. Have you ever been to Iceberg Alley? (Can Stock)

Since at least 1995, commercial iceberg harvesters have been used to collect pieces of icebergs. Commercial iceberg harvesting can involve wading out to collect chunks of the icebergs as they start to break up or going out on a boat with heavy machinery and breaking off chunks of the icebergs. Then, they use the iceberg water to make (and sell) things like:

- skincare products made from iceberg water, kelp, and other organic ingredients (Ossetra Wondrous Earth and East Coast Glow both make iceberg water–based products);
- beer and wine (Quidi Vidi Brewing Co);
- bottled water (Berg).

Fun Stuff

If you live in Newfoundland, you've probably seen plenty of these icy giants. If you plan to visit, why not check out some icebergs for yourself? Consider a boat tour and get up close and personal in a safe way.

79

Shelburne, Nova Scotia, has been hosting Whirligig Festivals since the late 1990s.

Did you have a spinning top when you were little? Or one of those sticks with a shiny, flower-shaped top that spun when you blew on it? If so, you already know what a whirligig is. Basically, a whirligig is any toy that spins or has a piece that spins.

In many places, folk artists make wooden whirligigs that end up being displayed on lawns instead of being played with regularly (although that happens too). In Shelburne, whirligigs are so popular that the town has devoted an annual festival to them. It's called the Whirligig and Weathervane Festival and it's packed with live music, whirligig-building workshops, and competitions for everything from Most Creative to Most Historical.

Fun Stuff

Want to build a whirligig of your very own? Visit the Dory Shop Museum on the Shelburne Waterfront on just about any Thursday from June to October. *www.shelburnemuseums. com/build-a-whirligig*

80

Danielle Fong started university in 2000—
when she was just 12 years old.

Scientist Danielle Fong was born in Dartmouth, Nova Scotia, in October 1987 and, just twelve years later, she enrolled at Dalhousie University in Halifax. For the next five years, she studied physics and computer science, while other people her age were in junior high, and then high school. When she graduated from Dalhousie in 2005, she left Halifax and went to Princeton University to earn a PhD in plasma physics, but left two years later when she realized that it was going to take her a very long time to make a difference in the world if she stuck with her original plan. So she decided to try and start a business instead.

She went off to Silicon Valley, California, where many of North America's biggest technology companies are based, and tried out a few business ideas, but none of them stuck—not until she started thinking about ways to use compressed air to create renewable energy. That's when she co-founded LightSail Energy, which is working to do exactly that. Danielle's idea could save a lot of energy, which is great for the planet. When you compress air, the process generates heat—and that heat creates energy. The interesting thing about compressed air is that you can also store it and use it later.

Fun Stuff

Can you think of a brand new way to save energy or reduce waste? Draw a comic strip that shows how your invention could make a difference for the environment.

Her company attracted some very important investors (people who give money to a company, and usually receive a percentage of the ownership in return), including Bill Gates, the co-founder of Microsoft and one of the richest men in the world. When this book was written, LightSail's air compression project had just started a twenty-year testing phase.

81

In 2000, a scientist discovered that a type of octopus living off the coast of Nova Scotia guards its eggs for up to 3 years.

Deep in the Bay of Fundy, there's a species of octopus called *Bathypolypus arcticus*—more commonly known as the spoonarm octopus or North Atlantic octopus. They're tiny creatures—the ones in the Bay of Fundy are as light as a golf ball and could fit nicely in the palm of an adult hand.

There are all kinds of creatures roaming deep in the ocean—like this spoonarm octopus—with many more still to be discovered. (Can Stock)

As you might have guessed by their common name, these little guys live in the North Atlantic Ocean. They can be found anywhere between 14 and 1,000 metres below the ocean's surface, but since they're deepwater octopuses, they're usually hanging around between 200 and 600 metres below.

Here's the most interesting thing about the spoonarm octopus. Most of the octopuses scientists have studied (mainly shallow-water species) live relatively short lives—males die right after they mate, and females only survive until their eggs hatch. And since it usually only takes between one and three months for those eggs to hatch, that doesn't leave the females much time.

Although there hasn't been as much research done, deepwater octopuses seem to have a different lifespan. Since the deepwater *Bathypolypus arcticus*'s eggs take almost three years to hatch, the females get to live much longer. It's not a very pleasant experience though—they stop eating as soon as they lay their eggs, and waste away while they wait for their eggs to hatch.

Fun Stuff

If you're at least eight years old, you're old enough to enroll in a PADI course that will get you on track to start exploring the ocean for yourself. Currently, in Atlantic Canada, only Torpedo Rays Scuba in Halifax seems to offer these courses.

82

In 2002, a Nova Scotia photographer opened an outhouse museum in his old high school.

Nova Scotia photographer Sherman Hines has taken pictures of a lot of different things over the years, from people and buildings to trees and sunsets. But back in the 1970s, Hines found something new (and old!) to focus on: outhouses.

According to a *Canadian Press* article, it all started when an elderly woman named Isabel Macneill hired Hines to take pictures of outhouses—because she was worried that someday soon, people wouldn't remember what they looked like. He took the job, which eventually led to published books on outhouses and, in 2002, an outhouse museum.

The Museum of the Outhouse is part of the Rossignol Cultural Centre in Liverpool, Nova Scotia, which was an old high school before Sherman Hines bought the building and turned it into a museum with lots of smaller museums inside. The museum has an outdoor section, where the actual outhouses are, and an indoor section, with small outhouse-related collectibles donated by Hines and other outhouse collectors.

Fun Stuff

Check out the Museum of the Outhouse and see it all for yourself. While you're there, make sure to explore the rest of the cultural centre as well—it includes a Wildlife Art Museum and a Folk Art Museum. *www.rossignolculturalcentre.com*

83

Kids in Summerside, PEI, have been learning about aerospace in school since 2005.

Ever wondered how airplanes really work? At Three Oaks High School in Summerside, the kids who want to know are getting all their questions answered—by taking classes in the school's aviation program.

The program includes two introductory classes where they learn how to use and take care of basic hand tools; safety in areas where airplanes are present; and the theory of flight. During the intro courses, they'll also practice things like working on a piston engine, inspecting and sometimes fixing actual aircraft, and even job-shadowing someone who works at an aerospace company. There's also an Aircraft Maintenance Orientation course—students who take this one spend most of their time working with local aviation and aerospace companies.

If you're wondering why kids in PEI are learning so much about aviation, you might be surprised to find out that aerospace is actually one of PEI's top industries. It's been growing ever since a Canadian Forces military base closed down in 1989 and the buildings and land were used for aerospace businesses instead.

Learn More

If you don't live in Summerside and you want to know more about aviation, you should definitely visit the Atlantic Canada Aviation Museum near the Halifax Stanfield International Airport. There's plenty to see; the museum collection includes a CF-5 Freedom Fighter, a CF-100 Canuck, an L-19 Bird Dog, and lots more. They also have helicopters and smaller airplanes.

www.acamuseum.ca

84

In 2005, it became illegal for anyone over 14 to trick-or-treat in Bathurst, New Brunswick.

Halloween changed for Bathurst kids and teens when, on December 19, 2005, Mayor Stephen Brunet and city clerk Lola Doucet signed a bylaw (a city law) stating, "No person(s) over the age of 14 yrs. shall take part in door to door soliciting (trick or treating) in the City of Bathurst."

This bylaw included a couple of other rules, too. At the time, no one (of any age) could wear masks or trick-or-treat at all after seven o'clock at night.

If you didn't obey the bylaw, you might have risked all of your allowance. Anyone who broke any of these rules could be fined anywhere between eighty and two hundred dollars.

A couple of years ago, a lot of people started talking about whether or not the bylaw was fair. In fact, according to a CBC News article, a Bathurst father emailed the current mayor, Paolo Fongemie, to complain about it. Other citizens interviewed by CBC supported the law, saying that seven o'clock is "a reasonable time"; one guy even said that he thought the age limit should be changed to ten instead of fourteen.

In September 2017, all that discussion made a difference. Although the bylaw is still in place, the age limit has been raised to sixteen, and the curfew has been extended to eight o'clock at night.

Fun Stuff

What do you think about the bylaw? Do you think it's fair? Why or why not? Write a short story or comic strip about one of these people:

- a kid who wants to wear a mask with their costume;
- a person who doesn't want kids to ring their doorbell after eight o'clock.

85

In 2007, a PEI farmer stumbled on a way to make cow farts (and burps) more environmentally friendly.

When PEI dairy farmer Joe Dorgan converted his farm to organic, he needed to find a new way to give his herd the minerals their diet required. He and his nutritionist discovered that sea plants (like seaweed) provided pretty much everything the cows needed. With plenty of beaches nearby, sea plants weren't hard for Dorgan to get—and they helped him save money.

He told CBC News that he was feeding his cows Irish moss, rockweed, and kelp. He had the mixture tested by an agricultural researcher named Rob Kinley (who was working at Dalhousie University at the time), and Kinley discovered something interesting. The burps and farts of Dorgan's cows produced twenty percent less methane because of their special seaweed diet. Since methane is an incredibly potent greenhouse gas, and a single cow produces as much greenhouse gas in a year as a car, this is a pretty big deal.

It gets better. After Kinley realized the seaweed caused the cows to produce less methane, he started testing other types of seaweed, too—some were native to Atlantic Canada and some were from Queensland, Australia, where Kinley works now. After testing all those different seaweeds, he found that one, a red seaweed called *Asparagopsis taxiformis,* reduced methane by eighty-five percent.

Ultimately, this could make a big difference in fighting climate change, but it will take some effort. Cows eat a lot—according to a *National Post* article, you would need to produce 1 million tons of seaweed a year to feed all the cows in the world. But there's hope—Kinley also says that amount is already being produced for human consumption.

Fun Stuff

Wondering what life is like on an organic farm? You can find out with a Farm Stay at TapRoot Farms in Port Williams, Nova Scotia. For a fee, you and your family can rent a cabin on the farm and spend your vacation exploring the orchards and fields. You can even help collect eggs or help harvest a crop.
www.taprootfarms.ca

86

The director of the 2007 animated movie *TMNT* was born in Moncton.

It was a while ago now, but you probably remember *TMNT*, the Teenage Mutant Ninja Turtles movie that came out in 2007. If you need a little help remembering, it was the one where a bunch of immortal monsters caused a lot of trouble by coming through a portal into the present-day world.

TMNT was also the first feature film about the Ninja Turtles made in fourteen years. And Kevin Munroe got to direct it. Born in Moncton in 1972, he would have been about thirteen when he first discovered a copy of one of the comics in a discount bin (that's right—the Teenage Mutant Ninja Turtles were a comic before they became a cartoon). This possibly influenced the darker take on the turtles that shows up in *TMNT*, since the comics usually had darker stories than the 1980s cartoon did.

Munroe used that same comic book in his pitch to direct the movie. When Munroe met with Peter Laird, one of the original co-creators of the franchise, he brought the comic book along to have it signed. When he opened the comic, he saw that Laird had written, "Dear Kevin, make a good movie—or else!"

That's how Munroe found out he'd gotten the job.

> ### Fun Stuff
> When the *Teenage Mutant Ninja Turtles* were first created by Kevin Eastman and Peter Laird in the early 1980s, it was more of a joke than anything else—they were just picking different parts of popular comic books at the time and mashing them all together to create the now-famous turtles. What kind of comic book character can you create?

87

In 2009, Halifax city council discovered just how bad the city's stray cat problem is.

Halifax has an astonishing number of stray cats. A 2009 report prepared by Superintendent William Moore of the Halifax Regional Police states that there could be anywhere between 40,000 and 94,000 stray or feral cats in Halifax. More recent reports put that number at around 60,000.

If you're surprised, there's a good reason for that. Feral cats are animals that were born outside and never had early contact with humans. As a result, they're scared of humans, so they become really great at hiding, even when they live in large groups called colonies. They're different from stray cats, which are usually lost or abandoned but may still be able to live with humans if they're adopted.

In March 2016, the Halifax Regional Municipality provided $50,000 to a group of local animal shelters so they could start a TNR (Trap-Neuter-Return) program. By trapping the feral cats, neutering them so they can't continue to reproduce, then sending them back to their colonies, the problem will eventually take care of itself (as long as the public does its part by taking good care of the cats they own).

Help Out

Want to do something to help the homeless animals in your community? Organize a bottle drive and donate the money to a local animal shelter. Talk to a parent about organizing one with a group of friends, or ask a teacher if you can set one up at school.

88

Acadia University opened a Robot Lending Library in 2011.

Visit a building with the word "library" on the front and you might find more than books inside. There are tool libraries (where you can borrow tools for a do-it-yourself project), seed libraries (where you can trade the seeds you have for ones you need), and toy libraries (never get bored of the same old toys again!).

In 2011, though, Acadia University—working with the Nova Scotia Community College (NSCC), Dalhousie University's Imhotep's Legacy Academy, Techsploration, and the Nova Scotia Department of Education—started lending something a little different: robots. Right now, the library owns more than eighty robots, including LEGO Mindstorms, EV3, and NXT robots, and lends them out to schools and youth organizations for year-long periods. There are a few rules, of course—you have to be using the robots to learn about science and technology, take good care of them, and have a robot-trained adult in charge, among other things—but if you're eligible to borrow one, it's a great opportunity, especially if you want to start a robotics team and compete.

Fun Stuff

If entering a robotics competition sounds like fun to you, consider getting a team together for FIRST® LEGO® League (FLL). The competitions are open to kids ages nine to fourteen, and there are a number of competitions across all the Atlantic provinces. For more information on starting a team, visit *www.firstinspires.org*.

89

In 2012, a dog named Bella saved her owner from a house fire.

At around noon on November 13, 2012, a man named Chris Larocque was making his lunch in Milton, Nova Scotia. His wife and kids were out—he was home alone, except for his puppy, a Bernese mountain dog named Bella.

A couple of years before, Chris had hurt himself in a car collision and his leg injury still causes him pain—he often walks with a cane, and when the pain flares up, sometimes it makes him fall down.

That's exactly what happened in 2012 when Chris opened the oven door to check on his lunch. He fell down, and the tea towel he was holding fell on the element (the hot part inside the stove) and caught on fire—and then the towel set the walls on fire. He called 911 on his cellphone, but then realized he couldn't get out of the house.

Luckily, Bella was there to save the day. When Chris called Bella she came to get him; he held onto her collar and told her to get him out. Bella hauled Chris out of the house and (except for a bit of initial running around) stayed with him until the ambulance and firefighters arrived.

In May 2013, Bella received a special honour for her bravery—she was inducted into the Purina Animal Hall of Fame.

Help Out

There are lots of animal shelters all over Atlantic Canada that need your help. If you're old enough, animal shelters are always looking for dog walkers and cat cuddlers!

90

In 2013, a tiny library in Cardigan, PEI, was declared the World's Smallest Library.

John A. MacDonald isn't just the name of Canada's first prime minister. It's also the name of the man who owns and runs Canada's smallest library, which is just 3.5 by 3.5 metres—it's probably about the same size as a bathroom in your house.

The tiny library is in Cardigan, which is on the eastern side of Prince Edward Island, near Montague, and it holds about 1,800 books. If you've got a spare five dollar bill, you can pay for a lifetime membership, and there aren't any late fines—you just have to promise to return your books.

MacDonald's hoping that someday his little library will end up in the *Guinness Book of World Records*, but so far he hasn't had any luck. Right now, there is no category for the world's smallest library. In 2013, however, MacDonald was successful in earning the title from another organization, called the World Record Academy.

Fun Stuff

If you live in PEI, get your parents to take you to Cardigan to check out the little library. If you don't, be sure to stop by the little building on Wharf Road next time you visit—it's definitely worth a poke around.

91

In 2013, a New Brunswick student received an award for fighting cyberbullying.

Every year, the Canadian Red Cross (a charity organization) gives out two Humanitarian Awards in each province—one for adults and another for youth, called the Young Humanitarian Award. In 2013, the New Brunswick Award went to Alisha Virmani, who had recently graduated from Fredericton High School.

Learn More

Hopefully you haven't been bullied, but if you have (or are), it's important to know what to do about it. Talking to your parents is a great place to start. You could also get advice from the Kids Help Phone by calling 1-800-668-6868 or, if you live in Halifax, you can talk to the Halifax Regional Police Bullying Hotline by calling 902-490-7283 or emailing *bullyhotline@halifax.ca.*

While Alisha was in high school, she was bullied—in person, but also online. This kind of bullying is extra stressful for people because it doesn't end when they leave school. As soon as the person being bullied turns on their computer or picks up their phone, they're vulnerable again—which means they never get a break from it.

When this happened to Alisha, she fought back by joining the Canadian Red Cross and eventually becoming a youth facilitator for their anti-bullying program, Beyond the Hurt. In 2010, she also designed T-shirts for Anti-Bullying Day. The shirts had the words "labels are for soup cans" on the back. And in 2012, she recommended changes to the NB Education Act that would help fight bullying. Her recommendations were accepted, and they're now a part of New Brunswick's legislation.

She started speaking out in high school, but she hasn't stopped. Now she tells her stories at conferences, including The Canadian National Human Rights Conference, RCMP Talks Conference, and the International Summer Course on the Rights of the Child.

92

A man reported a UFO in Kensington, PEI, in 2014.

John Sheppard from Moncton, New Brunswick, was camping when he saw something unusual—a flashing light in the sky over the water at Twin Shores Campground. In an interview with CBC News, Sheppard said that it looked like a spinning top or a dreidel.

Because he didn't know what the light was, Sheppard told CBC he tried to hide in some nearby bushes—but he still found the courage to film the light with his cellphone.

Sheppard uploaded the video to YouTube and when you watch it, you can see a single light flashing for a few minutes and then a second light appears and starts flashing as well.

When Sheppard got in touch with the Mutual UFO Network of Canada, an organization that studies UFOs, they weren't able to provide an explanation—which is unusual because they're really good at identifying flying objects (usually, they turn out to be a star or the International Space Station, according to the CBC article).

> ### Learn More
> Do you think there is life on other planets? Draw a picture of what you think an alien city would look like, and don't forget to think about:
> - what plants and vegetation might be like
> - what kind of technology they might have
> - what their atmosphere is like (is there gravity?)

It's also interesting that, in an interview with *Night Time Podcast*, Sheppard said he was contacted by someone else from Kensington, who saw the same lights on the same night as him.

Lots of people have made guesses, saying that it might have been a drone or a satellite, but so far the flying object remains unidentified.

NOVA SCOTIA

93

In 2014, the author of *The Nameless City* won an Eisner Award.

First of all, the Eisner Awards are really The Will Eisner Comic Industry Awards. They were created in 1988 to celebrate achievements in the North American comic book industry and have categories like Best Writer, Best Cover Artist, Best Webcomic, and Best Short Story. Because the comic industry in the US is gigantic, winning one of these awards is really, really exciting.

In 2014, Faith Erin Hicks, who lived and worked in Halifax for a number of years, won the "Best Publication for Kids (Ages 8-12)" category for her serial comic *The Adventures of Superhero Girl*. The main character of this award-winning comic is a superhero who can leap tall buildings and has super-strength. She also lives in Halifax, and has a lot of regular problems that even super-powers can't solve.

Since then, Hicks has been working away on other projects, including a series of graphic novels called the Nameless City trilogy (which is being made into an animated series as I'm writing this.

It's set to come out in fall of 2018—or has already started, depending on when you're reading this!).

> ### Fun Stuff
>
> Faith Erin Hicks has a bunch of great books written for exactly your age group, so if you like graphic novels, you should definitely pick up one of hers. For starters, try *The Adventures of Superhero Girl*, *The Nameless City Trilogy*, *The War at Ellsmere*, or *Brain Camp*.

94

In 2014, the town of Cape St. George tried to sell a dead whale on eBay.

Around the beginning of May 2014, a twelve-metre sperm whale washed up on a beach in Cape St. George, Newfoundland. Sadly (for the whale), it was either dead when it washed up, or it died when it was beached. Sadly (for the town), Cape St. George was responsible for disposing of the whale's carcass—an expensive and difficult task for a town that only has a population of 950 people. And the whale definitely had to be moved off the beach and away from the nearby houses because eventually it would rot, and the smell would be terrible.

The town tried to hire a local fisherman to move the whale with his fifty-foot boat, but the fisherman didn't think that even a huge boat like that would have enough power to tow away the whale. So, after holding an emergency meeting, they came up with a creative solution: auction the whale off on eBay in the hope that a museum might buy it. The deal: after paying for it, the buyer would also have to have the whale moved away from the beach.

The bids reached $2,025 before eBay noticed and removed the ad. It turns out that the town had violated an eBay rule that prohibits the sale of mammal parts. They also heard from the federal government. Since sperm whales are endangered, it's illegal to sell them—dead or alive. The last news reports state that the mayor of the town was hoping that if they offered the whale for free to the eBay bidders, someone might take it away. Luckily for all involved, the problem solved itself when, about a week later, the tide washed the whale carcass away.

Fun Stuff

It's pretty unlikely that you'll ever find a whale lying around on a beach, but you can always find lots of other interesting creatures. Next time you visit the beach, check out the tide pools and see how many tiny animals and insects you can identify.

95

A Prince Edward Island election was settled by flipping a coin in 2015.

Heads or tails? That was the big question on May 4, 2015, when Mary Ellen McInnis lost a Prince Edward Island election to Alan McIsaac by two votes. McInnis figured that someone might have counted the ballots wrong and asked for a recount, just in case there was a mistake the first time.

This time, the count showed a tie—Mary Ellen McInnis and Alan McIsaac had exactly the same number of votes—1,173 each. Now, here's where things get interesting. According to the Elections Act, if this election had been in Nova Scotia, the winning candidate would have been chosen by putting the candidates' names in a box, shaking it up, and drawing a name. If it had happened in New Brunswick, the returning officer (the person in charge of the election) would have chosen the winner. And if it happened in Newfoundland, they would have held a whole new election.

But in PEI, they flip a coin. Really. Look—here's the part of the Elections Act that says they have to do it: "Where it is reported to the returning officer pursuant to section 101 that an equality of votes is found to exist between candidates, the returning officer shall, in the presence of at least two of the persons authorized to be present under subsection 94(1), toss a coin to determine the winning candidate."

So that's exactly what they did. They gave heads to Mary Ellen McInnis, because when you put McInnis and McIsaac in alphabetical order, her last name comes first. Alan McIsaac was given tails, and when the coin was flipped, he won the job of MLA for Vernon River-Stratford.

Fun Stuff

Want to find out what an election is really like? Ask your teacher if your class can hold a mock election. You will need to choose people to act as politicians, who will need to create their own platforms (this means they'll decide what they'll do for the class if they're elected), and make signs for their campaign. Then your class will need to make up the voting rules, run the polls, and count the ballots. Who knows, maybe the winner will get to choose the next field trip.

96

In 2015, the tooth fairy started paying Atlantic Canadian kids less per tooth.

Atlantic Canadian kids unite—the tooth fairy has slashed the value of your baby teeth. In 2014, Visa Canada did a survey to find out how much money the tooth fairy was leaving under pillows across Canada, and they discovered something exciting: at an average of $3.46 per tooth, kids in Atlantic Canada were getting more than anyone else in the country. Compared to $3.21 per tooth in Ontario, $3.12 in Alberta, and $2.47 in BC, that's not bad.

But the results of the 2015 survey show the start of what could be an alarming trend: Atlantic Canadian kids are now getting the second lowest rate in the country per tooth, at just $2.79. (Kids from British Columbia get paid the least, $2.46 per tooth.) That's a big drop from $3.46 in 2014, and the national average of $3.44.

Learn More

Have you opened a bank account yet? It's a great idea to start learning about money early on, and there are lots of banks that offer free accounts to kids. Talk to your parents and see if it's a good time for you to transfer all that tooth fairy money from your piggy bank and into the real thing.

So what happened? When the survey was released, did the tooth fairy decide to correct the imbalance from the previous year? Or is Atlantic Canadian dental hygiene down, making quality teeth harder to come by? Unfortunately, we'll probably never know.

97

In July 2016, millions of moths plastered two New Brunswick towns.

Around the middle of the afternoon on July 23, 2016, people living in Campbellton and Dalhousie, New Brunswick, noticed something odd: there seemed to be more moths around than usual. By the evening, they were everywhere—news photos show the moths clustered around street lights, plastered over car windshields, and piled up on the ground. They even ended up in people's houses.

Dawn Kenny, who owns an inn in Dalhousie, told the *Canadian Press*, "They were everywhere and on everything. There were thousands and thousands of them. They were flying in the air in swarms, especially by the lights. Any place with lights, if you walked by, you'd have to push your way through with your hands to get them out of your face. There were so many of them."

At the time, there was a spruce budworm outbreak in Quebec (an outbreak is when something bad or unpleasant suddenly happens—like a lot of people in one area get a disease like measles, or millions of moths take over your town and get stuck to the walls in your house). Scientists think the spruce budworm moths were swept up by the warm air and carried to New Brunswick.

Fun Stuff

Feeling competitive? Grab a friend and two bug catchers (or just a jar with some holes in the lid) and go outside. Catch as many bugs as you can and then have a race to see who can identify the most bugs. Helpful hint: get a head start by checking out some books on insects from your local library.

98

In 2016, a lost 11-year-old boy used his iPhone to help his parents find him.

In December 2016, *CBC News* published an article about Josh Hopkins—a quick-thinking eleven-year-old boy who lives in Shelburne, Nova Scotia. According to the article, Josh got a new BB gun for Christmas and decided he wanted to try it out, so he headed into the woods with the gun, a pocket knife, and his phone. Unfortunately, he walked a little too far and got lost.

He could still use his iPhone, though, so he used Google to find out his GPS coordinates, which are a series of numbers that represent geolocation. Essentially, anyone who has your GPS coordinates should be able to find you. At this point, he only had two percent battery power left. Then, he texted the coordinates to his mom and told her he was lost. Later, he built himself a shelter and ate some spruce buds. He told *CBC News* they tasted terrible, in case you were wondering.

Fun Stuff

If you like to explore the great outdoors and you live in Nova Scotia, consider joining the Young Naturalist's Club. This free nature club for kids and their families will give you the chance to experience nature while learning how to identify plants and animals, keep a nature journal, and more. There are currently seven chapters across Nova Scotia. To find out more, visit *www.yncns.ca*.

While Josh was doing all this, his mom and dad gathered some neighbours and friends together and set out to find Josh. Six hours later, a neighbour named Tom Torak found him—and it was all thanks to Josh's quick thinking when he first got lost and decided to text his mom his GPS coordinates.

99

In 2017, PEI went missing from (multiple) maps of Canada.

At 5,660 square kilometres (and getting smaller—see Number 65), Prince Edward Island is a small province compared to, say, British Columbia, which is 944,735 square kilometres, or even Nova Scotia, which is the second smallest Canadian province at 55,284 square kilometres. But that's no reason to start leaving a Canadian province with almost 150,000 people off the maps—especially since the little province's population is growing faster than any other province in Canada.

But that's exactly what was happening in 2017, when the Hudson's Bay Company started selling T-shirts with a map of a PEI-less Canada printed on the front. Around the same time, the Vancouver Airport was selling a map of the world—as it would look if PEI didn't exist. To add insult to injury, an infographic created by CAA for Canada 150 also ignored PEI—they showed it, but forgot to give it any historic significance—which is odd, since PEI is birthplace of Confederation.

A lot of newspapers covered the missing province and the media coverage, combined with the social media outcry that followed, prompted the three companies to fix their mistakes. The Hudson's Bay Company stopped selling the T-shirts, CAA updated the online version of their infographic, and the Vancouver Airport map was fixed up, too.

Fun Stuff

Go to PEI! If you don't live there, that is. It's the perfect summer vacation spot with lots of beautiful beaches, delicious ice cream, and two fun ways to get there—you can either take the ferry or drive over one of the longest bridges in the world.

100

In 2017, someone found a Maud Lewis painting in a thrift store.

If you live in Atlantic Canada, you've probably heard of the folk artist Maud Lewis. And if you live in Nova Scotia, you've probably studied her paintings in art class. She passed away in 1970 (when she was sixty-seven), but decades later people still remember meeting her, and lots of people appreciate the colourful paintings she left behind of animals and coves, cars and boats. Recently, she even got her own movie, called *Maudie*, starring Sally Hawkins and Ethan Hawke.

Maud was very poor when she was alive, but she made enough to survive by selling her paintings from her tiny house in Marshalltown, just outside Digby, Nova Scotia. Now, though, her paintings are extremely valuable. So, imagine how shocked the staff at the Mennonite Central Committee Thrift Centre in New Hamburg, Ontario, was to find an original Maud Lewis painting in their donation bin.

In May 2017, the Mennonite Central Committee auctioned off the painting, called *Portrait of Eddie Barnes and Ed Murphy, Lobster Fishermen, Bay View, N.S.* It sold for $45,000, which the committee will put towards emergency relief, sustainable development, and peace-building projects.

Fun Stuff

Did you know you can visit Maud Lewis's house at the Art Gallery of Nova Scotia? When her beautifully painted house started to fall apart, people from the Digby community started fundraising to try and maintain it—but it got to be too expensive for them. The house was sold to the Halifax branch of the Art Gallery of Nova Scotia where it's on permanent display. *www.artgalleryofnovascotia.ca/ maud-lewis*

ACKNOWLEDGEMENTS

Whether they realize it or not, there are a lot of people who helped with this book. First and foremost, I want to thank the journalists, authors, podcasters, photographers, and videographers who do such a fantastic job of documenting history as it happens. I'd also like to thank the librarians, archivists, and museum curators who dedicate their careers to preserving that history, especially the people working at:

- The Maritime Museum of the Atlantic
- Halifax Public Libraries
- The Halifax Municipal Archives
- The Nova Scotia Archives
- The Provincial Archives of New Brunswick
- Memorial University
- The Rooms
- The Johnson Geo Centre
- Libraries and Archives Canada
- Historica Canada
- The New Brunswick Museum
- UNB Archives and Special Collections
- Prince Edward Island Sports Hall of Fame
- The Alexander Graham Bell Museum
- Nova Scotia Museum of Natural History
- National Gallery of Canada

I'd also like to thank the people who have supported and encouraged me in one way or another as I've written this book: Kat Kruger, Trevor Adams, Emily Pohl-Weary, Phil Moscovitch, Katie Ingram, Alison Delorey, Christy Ann Conlin, Janice Landry, Carol Bruneau, Lisa Doucet, Chris Benjamin, Jordan Boneparte, and Emily Amos. I really hope I didn't forget anyone, because I'm lucky to know so many wonderful, generous people it's hard to keep track. If I forgot you, I'm truly sorry, and please tell me so that I can give you extra thank-yous in my next book.

Thank you to Vicki King and Sebastien Sawler for helping me hunt for errors in my pre-submission draft. And thank you to Candida Hadley, who found time in her evening to read my intro and reassure me that it's worthy of publication.

Thank you to all the amazing people working at Nimbus Publishing—Terrilee Bulger and Heather Bryan for continuing to publish my books, Whitney Moran and Lexi Harrington for giving this book that oh-so-important second (and third and fourth...) look and for providing their valuable insight, and to Matthew McNeill and Karen McMullin for selling it. Thanks, too, to all the people working behind the scenes—there are people involved that I probably don't even know about.

Thank you to my parents, Cindy and Greg Steeves, and my in-laws, Sharon Barkhouse and Alex Verge, who are always happy to provide tidbits of information and take care of my kids. And most of all, thank you to Mike Sawler, who spends a lot of time listening to me ramble on about a wide variety of topics and still continues to support me in this whole writing thing, and to Simon and (again) Sebastien Sawler, for being awesome, inspirational people (with a high tolerance for motherly crankiness at deadline time).

Finally, thanks to everyone who read and recommended *100 Things You Don't Know About Nova Scotia*. You helped make this book happen.